PRAISE

For *Beyond Your Logo*

"Every business has a brand – the only question is whether or not that brand matters most to someone in need. In *Beyond Your Logo*, you'll learn how to intentionally make your brand a powerful driver of sales and profit."
-John Jantsch, author, *Duct Tape Marketing* and *The Referral Engine*

"In this detailed, practical book Elaine Fogel gives you the recipe for building a fully realized, differentiated brand that customers care about. Indispensable for small business!"
-Jay Baer, NY Times best-selling author of *Youtility*

"Elaine Fogel's book, *Beyond Your Logo*, provides a great amount of information with a mix of strategic thinking and tactical how-to's."
-Shep Hyken, customer service expert, keynote speaker, and *New York Times* and *Wall Street Journal* bestselling author

"*Beyond Your Logo* is a well-organized guide for small business owners. Elaine Fogel has broken her content into actionable bits giving readers manageable tools to develop their own customer-oriented marketing and branding plans. What makes this book so effective is that Elaine's seven brand ideas are achievable. Small business owners who read this can easily feel motivated to take action. Her concepts can serve as a long-term reference to help them reach greater success."
-Jeanne Bliss, President CustomerBliss and bestselling author of *I Love You More Than My Dog: Five Decisions That Drive Extreme Customer Loyalty in Good Times and Bad*, and *Chief Customer Officer 2.0: How to Build Your Customer-Driven Growth Engine*

"*Beyond Your Logo* by Elaine Fogel is a must read for entrepreneurs. Centered around seven key ideas, she walks the reader through clear, practical advice that spans well beyond branding and marketing into fundamentally important drivers in small business success – like being nimble and truly showing how your organization cares about the world. Those seeking to start businesses – or others who have already opened their doors – would be well served to spend some time reviewing Fogel's seven ideas, learning really important but often not difficult steps to take toward success."
-Rachel Hutchisson, Vice President, Corporate Citizenship & Philanthropy, Blackbaud, Inc.

"Elaine Fogel has written a much-needed guide for small businesses that want to attract and retain more customers but aren't quite sure where to focus. Her seven ideas cover important concepts that business owners can easily adapt to improve their companies' abilities to stand out and build a solid brand in their markets."
-Carol Cone, Chair, Edelman Business + Social Purpose

"Elaine Fogel's book *Beyond Your Logo* promises 7 big ideas that will matter to your small business and it's an absolute lie. There must be 250 incredible, pragmatic, and vital ideas in this book! Through storytelling, examples and quick to implement tips and tricks, Elaine's written a fantastic marketing primer that every small business owner should read and follow. Whether you're in your 25th year of business or just about to embark on your entrepreneurial adventure — you'll be a better business owner after reading this book."
-Drew McLellan, national branding and marketing expert, agency owner, columnist, author, and blogger for *AdAge Power 150* List blog, *Drew's Marketing Minute*

"Entrepreneurship is an often rewarding, yet challenging endeavor. One of the most critical parts of successfully starting and growing a business is getting your branding right, communicating it in a clear and consistent fashion with customers. Elaine highlights numerous important important aspects entrepreneurs must consider and execute in order to lay the foundation for long-lasting success."
-Omer Minkara, Research Director, Contact Center & Customer Experience Management, Aberdeen Group

Beyond your LOGO

7 BRAND IDEAS THAT MATTER MOST FOR SMALL BUSINESS SUCCESS

ELAINE FOGEL

For permission requests, contact the publisher:
Compass Press LLC
14001 N. 50th St.
Scottsdale, AZ 85254
602-380-7230
publisher@CompassPress.us

Special discounts are available on quantity purchases by corporations, associations, schools, etc. For more information, contact the publisher.

Published by: Compass Press LLC, Scottsdale, Arizona
Licensed images: CanStockPhoto, Vital Imagery, Vectorstock
Cover and interior book design by: Elaine Fogel

Publisher's Cataloging-In-Publication Data
(Prepared by The Donohue Group, Inc.)

Fogel, Elaine.
   Beyond your logo : 7 brand ideas that matter most for small business success / Elaine Fogel.

   pages : illustrations, charts ; cm

   Issued also as an ebook.
   Includes bibliographical references and index.
   ISBN: 978-0-9966613-0-0

   1. Branding (Marketing) 2. Small business marketing. 3. Logos (Symbols) 4. Success in business. I. Title.

HF5415.1255 .F64 2015
658.8/27

Printed in the United States of America
10 9 8 7 6 5 4 3 2 1

CONTENTS

PREFACE

Whether you own an existing small business, work for one, or are starting a new one, you'll definitely benefit from embracing *Beyond Your Logo: 7 Brand Ideas That Matter Most for Small Business Success.*

And why? Because mitigating risks and helping your small company succeed are the customary prime directives for most business owners and professionals. Goodness knows there are plenty of hurdles to overcome as it is.

When we look at the current state of small businesses in North America, we discover how prominent they are in our national economic engines. According to the US Small Business Administration's (SBA) "Frequently Asked Questions about Small Business" March 2014 report:

- There were over 28 million small businesses in the US (having fewer than 500 employees) in 2011.

- Since the end of the recession (from mid-2009 to mid-2013), small firms accounted for 60% of the net new jobs.

- Small businesses made up 99.7% of US employer firms.

- Over 72% of small businesses are sole proprietorships.

According to Industry Canada, there were just over 1.08 million small businesses with employees in 2012, with 55% having only 1 to 4 employees. Small businesses account for more than 98% of all firms and proportionally play a large role in net job creation.

Small businesses are the backbone of our capitalist societies. But there are inherent risks.

- About 10% to 12% of firms with employees open each year and about 10% to 12% close.

- Non-employer firms have turnover rates three times as high as employer firms.

- About half of all new establishments survived five years or more and about one-third survived 10 years or more. (SBA)

In Canada, 21% of new employer micro businesses (1-4 employees) failed after one year with 32% failing after two years. For small businesses with 5-99 employees, 15% failed after one year, with 14% failing after two years. (Industry Canada statistics, 2007-2009)

As tenuous as long-term business survival may be, the *2014 Wells Fargo/Gallup Small Business Index* reported that optimism among small-business owners had reached its highest level in six years. Additionally, more than eight in 10 US small-business owners said they would still become a small-business owner if they had it to do over again.

So if you're feeling as optimistic as these survey respondents were and want to increase your small business' chances for long-term survival and success, then this book is for you. Although many factors contribute to a company's success or failure, I focus on one major element – your company's brand.

Your small business may have excellent products and services, lots of investment capital, and an ideal location,

BUT if its brand is lackluster or nonexistent, success will be that much harder to attain. My intent with this book is to dispel the mistaken belief that a company's brand is its logo, look, and colors. It is much more holistic than that.

Your small business' brand emanates from the mindsets, attitudes, and behaviors of anyone and everyone involved in it. Every word, action, nuance, interaction, story, appearance, etc., has a profound impact on your customers' experiences. Since customers determine your company's brand reputation, it's critical that you do everything possible to ensure their experiences are amazing.

Good news... you don't need any marketing or branding knowledge or experience to benefit from these pages. Many of my recommendations are based on common sense – the kind that often gets overlooked in daily operations. I also explain all the marketing and branding terms and concepts I use in case you are unfamiliar with them.

I've divided the book into seven chapters (ideas):

Idea #1: A Strong Brand is Essential for Small Business Success

Idea #2: Put Customers at the Center of Every Action

Idea #3: Get Marketing and Branding Help When You Need Them

Idea #4: Professionalism Pays Off

Idea #5: Be Nimble. Be Quick.

Idea #6: Demonstrate Small Business Social Responsibility

Idea #7: Be Strategic

Please note that Idea #7 is the meatiest of all the chapters. This is where you get "down and dirty" developing your small business marketing and branding plan. I'll explain how to approach it when you get there.

So get ready to read *Beyond Your Logo: 7 Brand Ideas That Matter Most for Small Business Success* and learn the overarching concepts and tools that can take your company well *Beyond Your Logo.*

Several housekeeping notes:

- I use the word "customer" throughout the book to keep things simple. I realize that you may call your customers by other names such as clients, patients, patrons, students, members, etc. Let's start with the approach that whomever your business serves are its customers.

- As English is not a gender-neutral language, I alternate between male and female references.

- Please note that I have provided the names of companies, organizations, and websites in the book for reference purposes only. I encourage you to do your own due diligence before subscribing, using, or paying for any products or services. At the time of writing this book, I have no affiliation with these entities.

- Websites offered as citations and/or resources may have changed or disappeared between the time this was written and when it's read.

Thank you and enjoy the book!

Elaine Fogel

IDEA #1

A STRONG BRAND IS ESSENTIAL FOR SMALL BUSINESS SUCCESS

The US Small Business Administration mentions four basics of success in small business:

- sound management practices,

- industry experience,

- technical support, and

- planning ability.

What's missing? Your company's brand!

Your company can have all "four basics of small business success," but if it doesn't build and sustain a strong brand in its market, all the practices, experience, support, and planning can go nowhere fast.

A strong brand helps customers develop positive impressions and feelings about your business, which can influence how they'll act when it's time to make a purchase or take an action. Since the frequently used terms *brand* and *branding* are often misused or misunderstood, let's clarify them now so we're in sync.

There are a variety of definitions for these marketing words, depending on the source. If we took a poll of small business leaders, I'd bet that many would think that a brand is the logo or the look and feel of a business — its graphics, colors, and typography. Others may think it represents the names of products and services, like Pampers or VISA. But these definitions are only partly true.

The concept of branding goes back to prehistoric times when Egyptians branded their livestock. Its modern use can be traced to the late 18th and early 19th centuries, after the US introduced its first patent laws, and became more established with the passing of the 1946 trademark law.

Branding as a specialized area of marketing evolved during the late 1990s, when the late advertising copywriter and ad agency founder David Ogilvy coined this definition:

A brand is the intangible sum of a product's attributes: its name, packaging, and price, its history, its reputation, and the way it's advertised.

The definition was broadened by current business and marketing guru, Seth Godin:

Branding is the set of expectations, memories, stories and relationships that, taken together, account for a consumer's decision to choose one product or service over another. If the consumer (whether it's a business, a buyer, a voter or a donor) doesn't pay a premium, make a selection or spread the word, then no brand value exists for that consumer.

Small business marketing maven and bestselling author, John Jantsch, defined it in even simpler terms:

Branding is the art of becoming knowable, likable and trustable.

I agree with these definitions and expound on them. Basically, your small business' brand represents absolutely everything about it, whether you are its sole proprietor or are one of 200 employees. Yes, it's the visual representation — the logo, graphics, colors, look, and professionalism of a company's marketing communications materials or collateral. But it's also how employees represent the company — in their behavior, language, commitment, messages, facial expressions, and interaction with internal and external customers. It's also the promise your business makes to its customers and prospects and whether it overdelivers on these promises consistently and predictably.

Your brand is a combination of a customer's experiences with your business at every touchpoint. Each memory, thought, impression, website visit, story, sales letter, social media post, event, phone call, and transaction contribute to your company's brand reputation.

There's a common misperception that branding is reserved for huge corporations, the ones that have large enough budgets to build and sustain their brands. But that's a myth. Your small business needs to develop and maintain a positive brand, regardless of its size and budget. A powerful brand acts like a magnet, attracting attention and customers.

So what's in it for your small business? Why should this matter? Because there are many benefits to branding your small business.

Branding your Business

BENEFITS OF BUILDING YOUR SMALL BUSINESS BRAND

Building a strong brand for your small business can truly pay off. And the best part? Many elements of a strong brand don't have to cost much at all.

INCREASED VISIBILITY

Small businesses with strong brands typically have higher visibility in the locations they serve. Their relationships and stories can receive more local media coverage, increased word-of-mouth (WOM) referrals, and new inbound business leads. When prospects and customers come to your business, it can reduce the overall marketing and advertising costs of trying to attract them.

ABILITY TO ATTRACT AND RETAIN LOYAL CUSTOMERS AND EMPLOYEES

People gravitate to brands they know, like, and trust. Small businesses with strong brands are more likely to attract their target market segments (audiences) with less effort. Happy customers become repeat customers. They share their good experiences with their networks of friends, families, colleagues, and social connections, which can subsequently multiply.

Employees who work for businesses that have built and earned positive brand reputations — internally and externally — will stick around longer. That means improved retention rates with less aggravation, downtime, and cost. Higher retention rates also save business owners the time it takes to recruit, interview, and train new employees.

DIFFERENTIATION IN A CROWDED MARKETPLACE

When there are many other companies with similar products and services, stronger brands have an advantage over their competitors. If your customers are thrilled with your products and/or services, and your pricing is comparable with those of other businesses of your type, why would they switch? Your brand will stand out in their minds.

INCREASED CREDIBILITY AND LEGITIMACY

When a business has a solid brand, many will perceive it as having greater credibility and a positive reputation. Brand recognition and widespread exposure will often bring it brand legitimacy, even in the minds of people who have never been customers.

For example, I believe that Rolex has an excellent brand, regardless of the fact that I have never purchased or worn its watches. I perceive it as credible and legitimate without ever actually having a brand experience.

Here's another example:

Suppose you've heard of an excellent local restaurant but have never eaten there. Your friends have shared how much they enjoy the food and you've read articles and posts about the place. So when an out-of-town relative asks you to name a good restaurant in town, won't you recommend it?

Many of us have done this before. We feel confident in our referrals, based solely on the businesses' credibility and brand reputation.

EMOTIONAL CONNECTION

People who frequent well-branded businesses often feel an emotional connection with them. Whatever their rationale, whether conscious or subconscious, the emotional bond can keep customers coming back while they continue to refer others.

Take coffee, for example. People who can't live without their morning Starbucks coffee have emotional ties to the brand. For many of them, it's more than the beverage itself. Perhaps they relish the store environment, know the baristas personally, like the in-store merchandise, or get a warm feeling of community. Any or all of these experiences help build an emotional connection between the Starbucks brand and its loyal customers.

ABILITY TO FORM AND MAINTAIN LONG-TERM RELATIONSHIPS

When you serve your customers with consistent excellence, communicate with them regularly, and give them something they value, they are more likely to stay in the relationship for a longer term. As long as they continue to have positive brand experiences, they can become part of your business' circle of friends and fans.

REDUCED RISK

Well-branded small businesses are not as vulnerable to market shifts and economic downturns as those that lack strong brands. Although they may still experience customer attrition, they are usually better positioned to stay afloat and weather storms more capably than their counterparts can.

They also have an edge to earn back their customers' respect and patronage after receiving negative publicity or causing a poor customer experience. Loyal customers are often more forgiving with well-branded businesses. However, if negative experiences recur, then the risk increases.

INCREASED BUSINESS VALUE

According to David A. Aaker, ET Grether Professor of Marketing and Public Policy (Emeritus), University of California, Berkeley:

A company's brand is the primary source of its competitive advantage and a valuable strategic asset.

Strong brands have what we call, 'brand equity.'

 **Brand Equity:**

"The commercial value that derives from consumer perception of the brand name of a particular product or service, rather than from the product or service itself." (*Oxford Dictionaries*)

The same principle applies to your small business. The stronger its brand is in customers' eyes, the stronger the asset, and the more business value it acquires.

GROWTH AND INCREASED REVENUE

Of course, the best-case scenario for any small business is manageable growth with increased sales and revenue. Companies with stronger brands typically have greater opportunities to generate more money than those that do not focus on their brands at all.

It is widely acknowledged that strong brands enable businesses to generate a sales volume and price premium that improves revenues and margins. (Anastasia Kourovskaia, Vice President of Millward Brown Optimor

ELEMENTS OF A STRONG BRAND

Strong brands represent purpose, consistency, professionalism, commitment, and integrity. Whether your company has a unique selling proposition, or like many small businesses, it is similar to its competitors, it can stand out and build its customers' trust if it develops and maintains a strong brand based on some core elements.

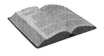

Unique Selling Proposition:

"The factor or consideration presented by a seller as the reason that one product or service is different from and better than that of the competition." (Entrepreneur Media, Inc.)

PURPOSE

What is your business purpose? Simply making money isn't enough of a driving force to thrive.

Making the world a better place may sound like a cliché but this noble objective resonates with so many people today, especially the Millennials (or Generation Y) born between 1981 through 1995. Now there's science behind this big-picture goal.

Jim Stengel, author of *Grow: How Ideals Power Growth and Profit at the World's Greatest Companies*, made a major discovery based on a 10-year global analysis of businesses that had grown far faster than their competitors had.

Leveraging the ideals of improving people's lives is driving the performance of the world's fastest-growing businesses.

Stengel cited these examples:

- Zappos, whose purpose is to deliver happiness through "wow" service;

- Dove, which exists to celebrate every woman's unique beauty; and

- Blackberry, whose goal is to connect people with one another and the content that is most important in their lives, anywhere, anytime.

Although these are big business examples, small businesses can adapt the same belief. A marketing colleague, Paul Chaney, whom I met virtually through our contributions to *MarketingProfs*, is a good example of living his small business purpose.

As principal of Chaney Marketing Group, he had spent years working as a social media marketing consultant, trainer, author, and speaker.

In the summer of 2012, he discovered that his passion for using social media for marketing was driven by more than just return on investment (ROI).

Return on Investment (ROI):

"A profitability measure that evaluates the performance of a business by dividing net profit by net worth." (Entrepreneur Media, Inc.)

Social media is a means by which people can connect in honest, transparent, authentic ways irrespective of borders. These connections may be virtual, but they are visceral as well. (Paul Chaney, 2012)

He felt a strong sense of mission to introduce social media marketing to emerging markets where its use was less known. That became his small business purpose and now it has attracted new business because of it.

The US Department of Commerce sent him to Ukraine in 2011 to present a series of full-day, training workshops to business people. Global technology companies have hired him to train their small business channel partners — many of which are located in countries like India and China, and regions like Eastern Europe and the Middle East. At that time, Chaney's purpose has opened up a new world of opportunities for his small business.

CONSISTENCY

What you and your employees convey to customers, suppliers, and prospects must be consistent. Why? To ensure that your company's brand — its name, identity, messages, services, products, etc., stick in their minds like glue. Keeping these things the same — day in and day out — builds brand awareness.

Have you ever tried to remember the name of a company or a product but it evaded you? Have you ever asked someone for assistance in a similar fashion to this: "You know... the one with the blue and silver packaging?" Or "the one with that cute kid in the TV commercial?"

As small businesses begin to capture attention, some brand elements start to stand out over others. People may remember one or two of the elements, and with more exposure, frequency, (market) reach, and consistency, the others can fall into place.

Market Reach:

"Estimated number of the potential customers it is possible to reach through an advertising medium or a promotional campaign." (BusinessDictionary.com/ WebFinance, Inc.)

Most of us have a favorite candy bar or treat we remember from childhood. If we're lucky and the product is still available, we don't have to reminisce; we can buy and enjoy it anytime. If we're even luckier, that delicious treat we recall so well tastes the same as it did when we were kids. Now that's product brand consistency!

Since brand consistency depends on all the moving parts of your small business, let's break them down one by one.

Consistent Brand Identity

Even though this book is called *Beyond Your Logo*, it is still essential to address your company's brand identity — the visual components such as colors, typography (the style and arrangement of text), symbols, and yes, its logo. These elements must appear consistently, no matter where you use them.

If you want your prospects and customers to recognize your company's visual identity, your logo can't be blue on Monday and purple on Friday. During my marketing career, I have unfortunately seen many brand logos and images used in substandard or inconsistent ways. Some typical missteps include:

Copying a logo from an electronic source (online) and using it in printed form. This causes the image to appear pixilated and fuzzy, resulting in an unprofessional impression. Digital logos are generally 72–150 dots per inch (dpi), a lower resolution than what is required for printing (300+ dpi).

Changing the logo design frequently. When you're trying to build brand awareness, using the same logo will help prospects and customers become familiar with it over time. This applies to the full-color logo and its black-and-white, grayscale, or one-color variations.

I know of one organization that changed its event logo each year. Its marketing department used the printed logo on T-shirts, brochures, direct mail pieces, banners, and other collateral, and the digital logo on its website. The problem was that it never gained any traction in branding the event. Small organizations have a hard enough time getting noticed; changing logos too often erodes their ability to cultivate brand recognition.

Copying and pasting a logo from one source to another. Each time you copy and paste a logo or image, it loses image quality. It's similar to photocopying a photocopy. With each new copy, the resolution and quality wane, affecting the output.

Most small business professionals don't have graphic design abilities, yet they still want the convenience of using their company logos in the documents they create. Since many small businesses use Microsoft® Word for word processing, here are the steps involved in importing your company's logo into your documents, using Word 2010 and 2013:

1. Go to the menu bar at the top of the page. Click "Insert."

2. Click the picture icon.

3. Open the folder and file in your hard drive where you store the high resolution JPG or PNG file and click it.

4. When the image appears, you can reduce its size by dragging in one of its corners. To make it larger, drag a corner out. One caveat... be careful not to enlarge the image too much or it may lose resolution and look pixilated when printed.

5. If you want to move the logo or image to the correct place, right click on the image and click "Wrap Text."

6. Select the most appropriate wrap for your requirements. Some wraps allow you to move the image anywhere on the page while others do not. Test each one until you find what works for you.

7. If you don't like the results, hit the "undo" icon at the top of the page in the Quick Access Toolbar — the one that looks like a curved left arrow. If that icon does not appear, click the down arrow to the right of that toolbar and click "More Commands." A window will appear with two columns.

8. On the left, in the Popular Commands column, scroll down until you find the "Undo" command. Highlight it and click the "Add" button in between the two columns. It will now appear in the right column. Then click "OK" to save the change. The "undo" icon will now show at the top of the Word screen each time you open the document.

Disproportionate logos or images. We've all seen them — logos that are stretched out of proportion. Don't they look awful?

Here's an example of my company's logo stretched out disproportionately and then the way it should appear:

If you import your logo according to my previous instructions and drag in one of its corners, you'll be able to resize the image proportionally.

Graphic designers and agencies usually supply clients with their final logos in an Encapsulated PostScript (EPS) file format, which they can send to advertisers and other designers for application. You can also ask them to send you high-resolution JPG and PNG files for your everyday printed documents, and lower-resolution GIF and JPG files for electronic media.

Consistent Name, Spelling, and Word Use

If your company name is long or doesn't easily convey its business, you may be tempted to use an acronym or shortened name format. But realistically, how will your prospects recognize it?

Try to keep things simple so you don't have to explain what your company does — whether in person or in marketing communications collateral. Companies like Nike, Apple, IBM, Intel, and other big brands have names that don't imply their products or services, but because they have huge marketing budgets and worldwide distribution, most of us know exactly what they sell.

Many small businesses have their principals' surnames or initials in their registered business names. Others have names that may be of significance to the founders but mean little to prospects and customers.

With limited funds to build your small business' brand name, it's even more important that you consistently use what you already have. If its name does not imply what the company does, consider developing a tagline that can help explain it.

Here are two examples I discovered online:

Totin Too, LLC in the Cranberry Township area of Pennsylvania is a small company whose name doesn't explain its service. So it has a tagline that does! "Cranberry Township Roofing Services!" Aha!

Cherry is a family-owned and operated business in Houston, Texas. Based on its name alone, one could guess that the founder's surname is Cherry or that the business has something to do with the fruit. Well, if you guessed the former, you are correct! The company's tagline captures its business: "Remove. Recycle. Return." It is a demolition and recycling company.

Many small businesses that sell a variety of products and services should ensure that everyone internally uses the same names, spelling, and terminology for brand consistency. For example, one of our small business clients, Payroll Experts, offers a service entitled: LaborExpert — Time & Attendance. To remain consistent, salespeople cannot write it as: Labor Expert — Time and Attendance. See the difference?

Other examples that require making choices:

- Roll Off Dumpsters For Construction Projects *or* Roll-Off Dumpsters for Construction Projects?

- High-speed Internet service *or* high speed Internet service?

- Web site services, website services, web site services, *or* Website services?

  Hint: Look for differences in upper and lower case letters, word spacing, and hyphens.

Consistent Messaging and Communications

With so many available communication channels today, small business professionals may find themselves overwhelmed. Among a company's website, blog, e-mails, printed direct mail, social media posts, salespeople, employees, traditional advertising, and mobile texting, there are so many places to ensure that messages and communications are not only effective, but also consistent.

An integrated marketing communications approach will help keep your business brand on track. It means aligning your company's messaging and communications across all your business' online and offline channels with clarity and consistency. Messages will have greater power and influence when words and images are uniform. Without this uniformity, your audiences can become confused, frustrated, or angry. Who wants that?

It's challenging enough to break through the din of the thousands of messages your audiences see each day. When your company's messages are clear, concise, consistent, and speak in one voice, there's a greater chance that more people will remember and act on them.

One way to ensure that the company (and anyone who represents it) sustains a consistent brand identity is to develop a written document or handbook of marketing communications or brand identity standards. This would include the company's typography, logo guidelines, colors, unique spellings, templates, paper stocks, and other details. You can launch the handbook in a fun way and provide an orientation for new employees, with periodic reviews to maintain integrity.

If the company has a fairly large number of employees, assigning the role of brand manager to one individual (and his team) will ensure that these standards are maintained in all external marketing communications. If the business has fewer employees or is a sole proprietorship, then the business owner or a contracted marketing consultant or agency can assume this responsibility.

Consistent Customer Service Communications

How you or your company's staff interact with customers is essential to building and preserving the business' brand integrity. Consistent communications also apply to the messages you and employees convey to prospects and customers during the sales process. What you say in a personal meeting with a customer should not differ from what you post on the company website or in social media.

For example, if your business offers a 90-day guarantee on a specific product or service, it cannot offer a different time period in its other communication channels. Contradictory messages can quickly lead to distrust.

To ensure consistency in customer service policies and messages, it's important to communicate regularly with employees so they are aware of any changes or new additions. In daily operations, I recommend using a customer relationship management (CRM) system where employees can record customer exchanges and notes.

Example:

On Monday, Jane told Mr. Jameson that she would reduce the cost of a heater from $129 to $99. When Mr. Jameson arrives on Tuesday when Jane is not there but Jeff is, he should have access to Jane's previous price promise. If he doesn't have a clue about what Jane promised the day before, then how will he know if Mr. Jameson's claim is valid?

A worse situation is when Mr. Jameson arrives on Tuesday and Jeff says he isn't aware of Jane's quote on Monday so he can't honor the lower price without checking with her when she returns to work on Wednesday! Would you want to be Mr. Jameson, standing there frustrated, debating whether it's worth returning or forfeiting the purchase to find another seller? This type of situation is far too common.

People who buy your products and/or services should have the same result whether you have one location or several. A Big Mac in North America looks the same, tastes the same, and weighs the same in any McDonald's location. It is this consistency that has helped McDonald's become one of the most recognizable brands in the world.

Another example:

Dr. Carmen Ramos is a chiropractor with two office locations in the same city. She employs two part-time receptionists — Casey in her west-end office and Simon in the east-end location.

Mrs. Calder, who was injured in a car accident, had been regularly seeing Dr. Ramos in the west-end office. Casey always greeted her warmly, inquired about her health, and asked for payment after her treatment was over.

When Mrs. Calder moved closer to the east-end location, she called and booked an appointment there. When she arrived the first time, Simon hardly looked up at her. When he asked her to pay the bill prior to the treatment, Mrs. Calder said she didn't have to do that at the west-end office. "Well, that's how we do it here," Simon replied.

Now that doesn't sound like a big deal, does it? But for Mrs. Calder, it just didn't sit right. She continued seeing Dr. Ramos in the east-end office a few more times. Simon never warmed up and still asked her to pay in advance. When a neighbor told her about his very nice chiropractor nearby, Mrs. Calder switched practitioners.

What are the chances that Dr. Ramos was aware of Mrs. Calder's reasons for leaving? Odds are few. If these types of situations continued, the chiropractor would be experiencing more-than-average attrition rates and making less money —all because of inconsistent employee behavior.

More on this in Idea #2.

PROFESSIONALISM

If you knew that a VIP was planning to visit your business, wouldn't you want everyone and everything to look first rate? If everyone in your business acts as if the next person they greet is a VIP or someone who's going to purchase the costliest product or service, it can help improve the company's level of professionalism immensely.

Ensure that your staff are presentable in appearance and that bathrooms, public spaces, and company offices are clean and tidy. On any given day, if a hot prospect walked into your location, would you be proud of your company's first brand impression?

When your employees communicate with customers and prospects, you can expect that they manage these relationships with a professional attitude, maintain a friendly and warm posture regardless of their personal issues, and represent your business professionally everywhere they go.

Ensure that the company's systems and operations resemble those of a larger business. Many technology tools are available that can help your small business look and feel like a top-notch, larger outfit.

In fact, one of the greatest rewards I experience is the surprise that people express when I tell them that my company is a boutique marketing agency. Based on the impressions they get from our online presence as well as telephone and e-mail interactions, they believe we are bigger. To me, that means our professionalism is leaving a positive brand impression.

More on this in Idea #4.

COMMITMENT

To achieve success, small businesses should commit to their brands emotionally, behaviorally, and fiscally (financially) over the long term. This means believing in and representing the company's mission, vision, goals, belief systems, brand promises, actions, and words.

Just as customers can become emotionally committed to companies as brand loyalists, your employees need to share a strong sense of commitment across the organization, whether there are three or 300 employees. Weak links in the ranks can erode your brand from within.

Company Mission & Vision

If your company has mission and vision statements, ensure you hire people who can commit to them wholeheartedly. Include them in your employee orientation programs and reinforce them throughout the year. Ideally, they should be part of employee evaluations as well.

- How well does the employee embody the company's mission?

- Is the employee aware of the company's vision and does she strive to achieve it?

Company Goals

If business owners and senior managers are the only ones privy to the company's strategic goals, how can they expect employees to commit to attaining them? When everyone is aware of these objectives and works together to reach them, both management and staff can celebrate their joint accomplishments. It is this cohesive approach that sustains a healthy work environment and a solid commitment to the brand.

Belief Systems

Belief System:

"A set of mutually supportive beliefs. The beliefs of any such system can be classified as religious, philosophical, ideological, or a combination of these." (*Wikipedia*)

In order for employees to commit to your small business' brand, they should ideally share the company's belief system. For example, people who are opposed to smoking cannot buy into a tobacco company's mission and belief system. Similarly, those who never read or value books won't make good brand advocates for a neighborhood bookstore.

For employees with a neutral stance, adopting your company's belief system can take time to nurture and sustain. When they feel part of an internal "family," are respected and appreciated, and their values are in sync with what they experience in the workplace, the more they can share mutually supportive beliefs.

Brand Promises

Brand promises communicate the value your products and/or services provide to customers and what they can expect from you. When you follow through on promises and ultimately wow your customers, they'll remember their experiences positively.

Brand promises also apply internally. When the company communicates its benefits for employees, it must live up to these promises. Otherwise, employees begin to lose faith in the internal brand. How then can they wholeheartedly commit to promises they make to customers?

That's why it's crucial that everyone – including business owners and senior managers – walk the talk, understand the company's brand promises, and then commit to embracing and modeling them.

Actions and Words

When employees are committed to your company's brand, their actions and words should be aligned. Developing an employee customer service manual can help reinforce expected actions and behaviors. Offering a comprehensive employee orientation program, followed by ongoing education, can empower employees to serve as brand ambassadors both internally and externally.

When you couple a handbook with employee recognition and reward programs, you can engage and motivate employees to present positive brand experiences even more.

More on this in Idea #2.

INTEGRITY

Integrity is at the core of any business culture. It incorporates essential fundamentals of business survival and is a key brand element.

Small businesses with strong brand reputations typically share the following characteristics:

- trustworthy
- honest
- transparent
- open to improvement
- ethical
- respectful
- law-abiding

A Positive Work Environment

When companies foster a favorable work environment and employees demonstrate a positive attitude, these usually show. A toxic or dysfunctional internal atmosphere can only create a staffing turnstile and negative morale.

Creating opportunities for open, candid dialog based on honesty, integrity, and respect should be part of the business culture. Honoring your staff will go a long way in building their commitment to your business. When raises or bonuses are unlikely or minimal, offer alternatives such as time off or flexible work schedules.

Say "thank you" frequently. Send handwritten thank-you notes or give out movie theater passes, promotional products, or other inexpensive appreciation gifts they can use. Their role in living the company's brand is vital. When you honor and respect them, they are likelier to feel positive about their jobs.

More on this topic in other sections.

Overdelivering on the Promise

Walking the talk and delivering what your company promises form the foundation of any strong brand. Whatever your company markets and sells must be reliable and of fine quality for the price. I say "for the price" because products and services vary greatly in both quality and cost.

If I buy an inexpensive pen for 50¢ at a small office and gift store, I may have different expectations than if I purchase a $20 pen. The 50¢ pen may not last as long as the $20 pen or may not look as attractive, but both promise to serve as writing instruments.

If the 50¢ pen outlives the $20 pen I had previously, then that brand has overdelivered on its promise and I'll be delighted. If the customer service I receive at the point of purchase is also amazing, I'll feel good, no matter which pen I purchase.

There's more on this in Idea #2.

IDEA #1 TAKEAWAY

Your small business can achieve greater success when the entire team recognizes the importance of branding and has a strong, continuing commitment to "live" the company brand every day. So if you started off believing that branding is for larger companies, consider this:

Your small business already has a brand — whether you recognize it or not. Wouldn't it be better to pay attention to it and make it the best it can be?

IDEA #2

PUT CUSTOMERS AT THE CENTER OF EVERY ACTION

Without customers, your business would not exist. It's that simple. Your business success and longevity depend on acquiring and retaining its target customers. You can't do so without developing and maintaining a customer-centric mindset.

So what is a customer-centric mindset? It's one that moves from selling products and/or services to serving customers' needs and engaging them as people individually, not as a collective or by customer number. It is a mindset that puts customers at the center of every action.

Before making business decisions or taking important actions, ask yourself, "How will this affect our customers?" Then make the best decisions you can, given your company's financial and human resources.

In the age of the customer, executives don't decide how customer-centric their companies are — customers do. (Kate Leggett, "Navigate the Future of Customer Service in 2014," *Kate Leggett's Blog*, Forrester Research, Inc.)

Before we dig any deeper, let's identify the different types of customer-related definitions:

CUSTOMER-RELATED DEFINITIONS

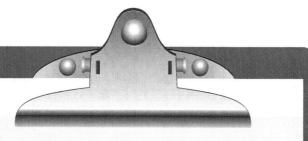

Customer Engagement:
Represents "the ongoing interactions between company and customer, offered by the company, chosen by the customer." (Paul Greenberg, *HubSpot Blogs,* 2014)

Customer Experience:
Represents "the sum-totality of how customers engage with your company and brand, not just in a snapshot in time, but throughout the entire arc of being a customer." (Adam Richardson, "Understanding Customer Experience," *Harvard Business Review,* Oct. 28, 2010)

Customer Journey:
"The complete sum of experiences that customers go through when interacting with your company and brand. Instead of looking at just a part of a transaction or experience, the customer journey documents the full experience of being a customer." (Audra Sorman, *SurveyMonkey Blog,* 2014)

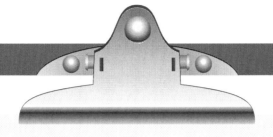

Customer Loyalty:
"The level of faithfulness shown by a customer in continuing to purchase a particular product or brand." (Monash University, Business and Economics)

Customer Orientation:
"The belief that customers and their perspectives are of the highest value and consequence in an organization." (Customer Service Psychology)

Customer Relationship Management (CRM):
"A system for tracking customer behavior for the purpose of developing marketing and relationship-building processes that bond the consumer to the brand." (BrandChannel)

Customer Touchpoints:
"Represent every place, experience, and person with which/whom customers interact with your business." (Elaine Fogel)

THREE CUSTOMER TYPES

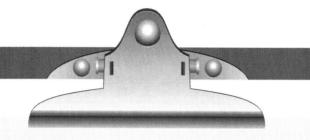

Internal customers are people with whom you work internally to do your job. These can include coworkers, bosses, suppliers, and any external consultants or outsourced individuals who work for the company.

External customers are outside companies or individuals who purchase products and/or services from your business. For business-to-consumer (B2C) companies, customers are consumers. For business-to-business (B2B) companies, customers are those who work for the businesses that purchase products or services from your company.

Referral sources are the individuals, agencies, businesses, and organizations responsible for referring others to your company. These can include current or previous customers, current or former employees, suppliers, bloggers, your social media network, friends, family members, neighbors, etc. This group can include the influencers and brand ambassadors who can greatly affect your business success.

CUSTOMER SERVICE — THE HEART OF A CUSTOMER-CENTRIC BRAND

At the heart of a customer-centric business is customer service — how your company manages its customer relationships, both internally and externally. What will success look like when you do this well?

The superlative outcome in external customer service is when customers have memorable brand experiences, return to buy again, and then rave about your business to others. The outstanding result in internal customer service is when employees enjoy their jobs, take pride in their work, achieve their potential, feel valued and appreciated, stay longer, and rave about your company to others.

If you've ever doubted the significance of customer service excellence to your business brand, browse through the following statistics. Keep in mind that most of these survey results represent large companies.

B2C CUSTOMER SERVICE STATS

- 65% of respondents stopped using a brand's products or services because of a poor customer experience. (*Parature 2014 State of Multichannel Customer Service Survey*)

- Customers who had the best past experiences spend 140% more compared to those who had the poorest past experience. (Peter Kriss, *Harvard Business Review*, 2014)

- 81% of prospective buyers were frustrated because the company doesn't make it easy to do business with them. ("The $6 Trillion Opportunity: How Digital Can Improve Customer Experience to Drive Revenue Growth," Accenture Strategy, 2015)

- 53% of US consumers switched service providers due to poor customer service experiences. ("The $6 Trillion Opportunity: How Digital Can Improve Customer Experience to Drive Revenue Growth," Accenture Strategy, 2015)

- 84% of customers were frustrated by companies promising one thing but delivering another. ("The $6 Trillion Opportunity: How Digital Can Improve Customer Experience to Drive Revenue Growth," Accenture Strategy, 2015)

- 81% of customers who switched claimed that companies could have done something to prevent them from switching: 72% said that resolving their issue in the first contact would have been effective; 48% reported that recognizing and rewarding them for doing more business with the companies would do the trick; another 48% mentioned that contacting them proactively to let them know about ways to enhance their experience with companies would work. (*Accenture 2013 Global Consumer Pulse Survey*)

- Only 5% of consumers said that the customer service experiences they have with companies usually 'exceed their expectations.' (*American Express® 2014 Global Customer Service Barometer*)

- 29% said that companies usually 'miss their expectations' for customer service. (*American Express® 2014 Global Customer Service Barometer*)

- More than nine in ten consumers talk about their good customer service experiences, at least some of the time (93%), while 46% tell someone about them all of the time. (*American Express® 2014 Global Customer Service Barometer*)

- When it comes to poor customer service experiences, nearly all (95%) consumers talk about them, with 60% reporting that they talk about these experiences all of the time. (*American Express® 2014 Global Customer Service Barometer*)

- Over two thirds (68%) of consumers state that they are willing to spend more with a company they believe provides excellent customer service. (*American Express® 2014 Global Customer Service Barometer*)

- 60% of consumers who intended to conduct a business transaction or make a purchase, decided not to due to a poor service experience. (*American Express® 2014 Global Customer Service Barometer*)

Here's good news for small B2C businesses:

- US consumers are choosing small businesses because of the personalized experiences they provide compared with larger businesses. ("Consumers Favor Small Businesses Because of Their Customer Focus," eMarketer.com, April 21, 2014)

- Nearly all (94%) US consumers say that shopping at small businesses makes them "feel good." (*Small Business Saturday Consumer Insights Survey*, 2014)

- Two-thirds (66%) of consumers say the main reason they patronize small businesses is because they value the contributions they make to their community. (*Small Business Saturday Consumer Insights Survey*, 2014)

- More than half (57%) say they know one or more of their local small business owners personally. (*Small Business Saturday Consumer Insights Survey*, 2014)

- Almost half (49%) of those surveyed said that small, independent businesses provide the best customer service; only 11% picked large companies. (Brandon Knight, "Customer Service: A Market Differentiator For Small Business," *Huffington Post*, October 14, 2014)

- Even though these statistics focus on the B2C sector, there are lessons here for B2B companies, too.

B2B CUSTOMER SERVICE STATS

Participants ranked customer service as the #1 factor impacting vendor trust.

- 95% of B2B customers shared bad experiences and 87% shared good experiences with others.

- 62% purchased more after a good customer service experience.

- 66% stopped buying after a bad customer service interaction.

- 69% attributed their good customer service experience to a quick resolution of their problem.

- 39% continued to avoid vendors two or more years after a bad experience.

  (All of the above: *Zendesk/Dimensional Research, Customer Service and Business Results, 2013*)

- 83% of B2B buyers either agreed or strongly agreed that an excellent customer service experience would lead to them purchasing again from the same supplier. (Accenture/hybris "Building The B2B OmniChannel Commerce Platform Of The Future" November 2014)

Because internal customer service is linked to employee engagement, I will address internal customers in the next section.

CUSTOMER ENGAGEMENT — THE SOUL OF A CUSTOMER-CENTRIC BRAND

What is customer engagement?

It's about creating long-term value that encourages customers to continue interacting with your brand in ways that matter to them, not you. You can't be selfish and you have to think well beyond the next quarter or year. It's all about creating meaningful value that encourages them to continue to build a relationship with your brand. (Rohit Bhargava, quoted in "Redefining Customer Engagement: Ogilvy Marketing Executive Rohit Bhargava on Why Modern Marketing Tactics Mostly Come Up Short," Josh Zywien, OpenSource Labs)

Engagement is the emotional bond or attachment that a customer develops during the repeated and ongoing interactions accumulated as a satisfied and loyal customer. When customers are engaged with an organization, they are emotionally connected, passionate about its products and services, as well as aligned with the purpose and direction of the organization. (Adam Edmunds, "Digging Deeper: How Emotions Drive Customer Choices," *Allegiance E-Commerce Times*, November 22, 2008)

EXTERNAL CUSTOMER ENGAGEMENT

According to Edmunds, there are four primary drivers of customer engagement. These drivers apply to nearly all industries, and are present in every business relationship. They are the foundation of how customers rate their emotional bond with a business.

They include:

1. feeling protected,
2. feeling confident and informed,
3. feeling valued, and
4. helpful service.

According to 2013 research by Gartner, Inc., "Engaged customers are usually better advocates of the brand and are more loyal and more profitable."

So what should your small business do to ensure it is engaging its customers at every touchpoint?

In the April 2014 issue of *CRM Magazine*, Sarah Sluis' article, "The 4 Pillars of Responsible Customer Engagement," provides the answers:

1. **Relevance**. Relevance is about understanding the customers and using information about them appropriately, which requires mapping the customer journey. This means walking in your customers' shoes and evaluating every process and interaction to ensure efficient operations without gaps.

   It also entails providing customers with relevant, timely, and useful information. (My comment)

2. **Respect**. Respecting customers means using "organizational empathy" as a guiding force. "If you think about empathy at an individual level, it's a human's ability to understand, without explicit feedback, the needs of another person."

   An employee who is treated with respect and understands the company's mission is more likely to pass that attitude on to the customer.

3. **Credibility**. Credibility comes down to delivering on brand promises. With consumers constantly evaluating a company's ability to do so, consistent interactions are critical to finding and keeping customers.

4. **Value**. Good customer experiences are not about discounts or offers but about developing long-term, loyal relationships with customers by giving them good value.

   This means being helpful, informative, and accommodating, focused on customers' needs before profits. (My comment)

So what does it look like when a company firmly grounds its four pillars and responsibly engages with consumers? Messages reach a customer how, when, and in the channel she wants... Customers know they're with a brand that delivers on its promises. (Sarah Sluis)

When you tackle your business' Marketing & Branding Plan in Idea #7, you'll want to incorporate these four pillars into your customer engagement tactics.

INTERNAL CUSTOMER (EMPLOYEE) ENGAGEMENT

What is employee engagement?

People want to come to work, understand their jobs, and know how their work contributes to the success of the organization. (John Baldoni, "Employee Engagement Does More than Boost Productivity," *HBR Blog Network*)

Studies show that engaged employees are more productive, have enthusiasm for their companies' success, have improved quality of work and health, have a lower turnover rate, are more satisfied at work, and contribute to better financial returns for the companies that employ them. Yet there's still room for improvement.

- Close to a quarter (24%) of employees are disengaged, and another 36% can be described as either unsupported or detached. (*2014 Global Workforce Study*, Towers Watson)

- A full 60% of employees lack the elements required to be highly engaged. (*2014 Global Workforce Study*, Towers Watson)

- Nearly two out of 10 employees are actively disengaged. These employees do not say positive things about the company, do not see a long-term path, and do not strive to go above and beyond. (*2015 Trends in Global Employee Engagement*, Aon Hewitt)

- Just over a quarter (26%) of employees say they are likely to leave their employer within the next two years. (*2014 Global Workforce Study*, Towers Watson)

The Aon Hewitt *2015 Trends in Global Employee Engagement* also indicates that:

- Although employee engagement in North America is on the rise (66%), there is deterioration in employee perceptions of empowerment, autonomy, and growth.

- A relatively large number of employees (68%) say positive things about their company, but fewer see a long-term future with their company or deliver their best performance every day.

- About half of employees have a favorable view of the top engagement drivers—career opportunities, reputation, and pay – which are so critical to their engagement.

It pays to have better customer experiences (CX) and engaged employees, according to Temkin Group's *Employee Engagement Benchmark Study*, 2015:

- Compared with disengaged employees, highly engaged employees are 2.5 times as likely to stay at work late if something needs to be done after the normal workday ends, more than twice as likely to help someone at work even if they don't ask for help, more than three times as likely to do something good for the company that is not expected of them, and more than five times as likely to recommend that a friend or relative apply for a job at their company.

- Companies that outpace their competitors in CX have 50% more engaged employees than those with CX that lags their peers.

And, some good news for small business:

- About 60% of employees in companies with 100 employees or less are moderately or highly engaged compared with only 49% of employees at companies with more than 10,000 employees. (*Employee Engagement Benchmark Study*, Temkin Group, 2014)

- 63% of employees at small businesses say they are extremely or very satisfied with their job. (*2015 Aflac WorkForces Report,* Small company business trends)

These statistics tell us that some companies have not been investing in their most valuable asset — their employees. It's possible, of course, that the recession and the slow economic recovery have taken a toll on training and development budgets. However, whatever costs are associated with managing employees, giving them feedback and encouragement, and ensuring that they are on the same page with the company's objectives are worth every penny in the long run. There's always a high cost in recruiting and training new workers.

So what will it take for your small business to engage its employees and keep them motivated? Of course, offering fair compensation and benefits is a biggie, but aside from this, the areas required to lift engagement for front line non-management and professional employees are centered on an aligned package of development, rewards and recognition.

Bottom line? Investing in employee engagement will pay off big time for your small business.

TOP 10 BENEFITS YOUR SMALL BUSINESS CAN GAIN BY ADOPTING A STRONG CUSTOMER-CENTRIC MINDSET

1. BUILDS TRUST, CREDIBILITY, AND SOLID REPUTATION

When you serve and engage customers with excellence, delivering on the company's promises consistently, they will gradually develop a reason to believe in your business brand. Your company will gain customers' trust and confidence and increase its level of credibility and reputation.

2. INCREASES WORD-OF-MOUTH REFERRALS

Building on #1, the more that customers trust your business, the more they will refer it to friends, family, colleagues, and their online networks.

3. GIVES YOUR BUSINESS A COMPETITIVE ADVANTAGE

When your company is customer centric, and customers talk about it positively, its brand can rise to a top-of-mind position, giving it a distinct edge over its competition.

4. REDUCES EMPLOYEE STRESS AND FRICTION

When there are clear-cut, customer-centric standards that all employees believe in and follow consistently, they'll know what to do and when. These guidelines can lessen confusion and customer mess-ups and in turn, greatly reduce employee friction and stress. Additionally, a company that honors its employees will have a happier staff who respect one another and play nicely in the sandbox.

5. REDUCES CUSTOMER ATTRITION

When your business puts customers first (internal and external), it increases its ability to retain them. As long as customers continue to see the value of patronizing or working for your business, they can become brand loyal and stick around longer. In other words, you'll experience less attrition.

6. SAVES MONEY

When your small business maintains a strong customer orientation and mindset — internally and externally — employees stay longer in their jobs, thus reducing company costs to recruit and train new ones.

When customers rave about your business and continuously refer new customers your way, the company can often adjust its marketing budget to reflect these inbound leads. It takes more marketing and advertising dollars to acquire new customers than to wow the current ones.

7. INCREASES CUSTOMER RETENTION AND LOYALTY

Customer loyalty can bring big benefits to small businesses. Existing customers not only comprise the majority of top line revenue, but can dramatically affect a business' bottom line. It can cost up to ten times more to acquire a new customer than to retain an existing one. ("Achieving Big Customer Loyalty in a Small Business World," *Manta & BIA/Kelsey Customer Loyalty Surveys, 2014*)

Many factors are at play in determining your company's customer retention rate. Price, quality, expertise, loyalty programs, location, etc., can all affect the outcome. You can control some of these aspects but not others, such as the cost of raw materials, infrastructure, wholesale goods, and service equipment and tools.

However, when your business is consistently customer centric, wowing and engaging customers, there's a greater chance that they'll stay and become brand loyal. Periodically ask customers why they patronize your business. What you discover can help identify the effects of being customer oriented.

8. REDUCES RISK AND IMPROVES SUSTAINABILITY

As stated in #5, when your business treats all its customers exceptionally well and with respect, it can reduce its risk for attrition. Brand-loyal customers who value your company and people may be less inclined to jump ship when your competitors entice them with attractive "carrots." Since customer retention is a vital contributor to sustainability, your business is in a better position to weather economic downturns, crises, and other business threats.

9. LEADS TO GROWTH

When your business develops a solid brand reputation for being customer centric, it can entice more inbound leads, referrals, and buzz, enabling it to grow. Because people are attracted to success, the company can experience even more growth opportunities.

10. INCREASES REVENUE AND PROFITS!

When your company adopts a customer-centric mindset and other business factors are relatively stable, it can improve its success, generating more money and profits.

Now that you've become aware of the true benefits of operating a customer-centric business, it's time to begin the paradigm shift or "mindset adjustment" that can help you achieve it.

3 TYPES OF CUSTOMER SERVICE

To simplify things, I have segmented customer service into three types.

Inferior service is when a company (or its employees) demonstrates some or all of these characteristics and behaviors:

- shows little to no genuine concern for, or interest in, customers or their needs;

- exhibits unavailability or inaccessibility to customers;

- responds to customers poorly or late;

- demonstrates unfriendly, unapproachable, or inappropriate behavior;

- presents a poor image (inappropriate attire, sourpuss face, unsuitable tone of voice, etc.);

- manifests an inability to handle customers' problems or complaints;

- acts too pushy by upselling or pressuring customers;

- blames others for mistakes;

- makes excuses why they can't fulfill customers' expectations;

- overpromises and underdelivers; and

- lies or tells customers what they want to hear.

Based on your own experiences as a customer, I bet you can add to this list. These inferior customer service behaviors cause dissatisfaction and disappointment, resulting in negative word of mouth, poor reviews, and attrition.

This issue brings us to satisfactory service – what marketers used to consider the ideal type, but no longer.

Satisfactory service is when customers think their experiences were OK or fine. Other descriptors that come to mind: average, reasonable, adequate, passable, and acceptable.

Whenever I run into a gas station for a cup of coffee, I help myself, approach the cash register, pay, and leave in less than five minutes. Sure, the cashier may greet me or smile, but overall, my experience is average. Since I don't expect more than that, I walk away a satisfied customer.

Will I return to that station for coffee? Maybe or maybe not. It depends on many other factors such as where I am, the time of day, my urge for coffee, and convenience.

However, when a business provides exceptional service, that's when memorable experiences happen.

Exceptional service is when your business "blows customers away" by going above and beyond their expectations. In order to achieve this superlative, you and your employees do the following:

- amaze
- astound
- awe
- dazzle
- delight
- enchant
- knock out
- surprise
- WOW!

Such an awesome experience happened to me when I visited Dutch Bros. Coffee for the first time. Maybe you've never heard of this company – it has 200 company and franchised locations in only seven US states: Oregon, California, Washington, Idaho, Nevada, Colorado, and Arizona. However, I wouldn't be surprised if one day, it will be as ubiquitous as Starbucks. The reason? They make customer experiences amazing!

When I pulled up to the drive-through window of the small hut-like building, the three employees inside all greeted me with smiles and hearty welcomes. They engaged me in friendly conversation, and when they heard that it was my first visit, well, the red carpet turned ruby!

The employee at the window – let's call her Susan – asked my name and told me hers. She asked questions and advised me on the types of coffee that would meet my taste preferences.

When I told her that I liked my soyamilk-to-coffee ratio 2:1, Susan enthusiastically suggested the soya latte, assuring me that I'd really like it. In a flash, the cost jumped from $2.60 to $4.25 and I didn't flinch a bit.

When I reached for a stevia packet in my purse, she said I could save it. They had stevia in stock all the time! I hadn't previously seen stevia sweetener in any other coffee shop chain.

Susan explained the company's loyalty card program, which I declined, indicating that I work from a home office and wouldn't be stopping by that frequently. But that wasn't a problem for her.

She said I could come by any time and handed me a new loyalty card with all but one box left to fill out! I pulled away with my coffee and loyalty card in tow, smiling broadly.

Now I ask you... what did that take? A powerfully positive attitude, exceptional customer service and orientation, and employee empowerment to make customers' brand experiences amazing.

What would a similar experience cost your company? Nothing, after developing a solid customer-centric culture and some staff training, which many businesses do anyway.

It's not surprising then, why J.D. Power and Associates ranked Dutch Bros. Coffee the highest in customer satisfaction, compared to other coffee companies, in its 2012 Specialty Coffee Retailer Satisfaction Report. The company's philosophy says a lot about its culture, too:

Dutch Bros. Coffee has always focused more on people than the bottom line, with a desire to transform lives rather than conduct transactions.

Now get this. The company started small as a single espresso pushcart, operated by dairy farmer brothers Dane and Travis Boersma, in the small town of Grants Pass, Oregon, proving that success comes to companies that put customers first. Its "Dutch Creed," posted online, sums up its customer-centric mindset:

Here at Dutch Bros., we're all about being positive and lovin' life. That's why when we came across the Optimist's Creed, we decided to adopt it as our own and call it the Dutch Creed. We strive to pass the good vibes on to our employees and customers through leadership within our company, and customer service. Check it out; it just might change your state-of-mind:

To be so strong that nothing can disturb your peace of mind.

To talk health, happiness and prosperity to every person you meet.

To make all your friends feel there is something in them.

To look at the sunny side of everything and make your optimism come true.

To think only the best, to work only for the best and expect only the best.

To be just as enthusiastic about the success of others as you are about your own.

To forget the mistakes of the past and press on to the greater achievements of the future.

To wear a cheerful countenance at all times and give every living creature you meet a smile.

To give so much time to the improvement of yourself that you have no time to criticize others.

To be too large for worry, too noble for anger, too strong for fear, and too happy to permit the presence of trouble.

Your small business can also achieve this customer-centric "Nirvana."

MANAGING EXTERNAL CUSTOMERS

Have you ever heard someone say something like this?

"If we could only get rid of our customers, I'd really love my job."

Say this to a group of small business owners and their employees, and I'd bet you'd see a lot of heads nodding in agreement. No one said that dealing with people would be easy. But when owners and employees believe that their customers are an annoyance or a pain in the butt, they need to take a long hard look at why they're in business altogether.

Your customers figuratively put food on your (and employees') tables. Some of them will be a breeze to deal with, while others will test your patience.

The first step in managing external customers is accepting that they are individuals just like your family and friends — people with strengths, flaws, personalities, sense of humor (or lack thereof), and idiosyncrasies. Does that change things for you?

Maybe it seems simplistic, but that's because it's basic! If you can have compassion and tolerance for your family members — when they're at their best and at their worst — you can manage customer relationships. In fact, customer relationships will probably be easier to handle!

If dealing with people isn't your particular strength, then you have three options:

1. Take a series of customer service workshops, practice, and improve. Changing your paradigm is essential.

2. Consider having other people work the front end of the business.

3. Get a job tending sheep in New Zealand!

WHAT NOT TO DO

DON'T lose focus on caring about customers.

All it takes is letting one's guard down once and a company can lose potential business in a heartbeat. Making customers wait unnecessarily, not communicating with them, ignoring them, or being unavailable can contribute to business death. Plus, they won't be coming back!

DON'T respond late – or never.

I've been at the receiving end of such indifference on numerous occasions. I've called businesses that others have referred or I've met the principals at networking events. I've left voicemails and sent e-mails and received no replies.

Whether intended or not, this behavior sends me a strong message that these companies don't really want my business; they must have plenty of customers already. How foolish is that?

If your business is up to its ears in orders or work and you cannot handle new customer requests, don't ignore the prospects who have shown interest! Show that you care and be honest with them. Tell them how swamped your company is right now, suggest a later date if possible, or refer them to another provider. (Yes, a competitor!)

Prospects will respect your candor and may even refer your company to others. They may also return at a time when your business is slower and you can accommodate them then.

One way to manage your company's ebbs and flows is to anticipate busy seasons and growth spurts. Plan for them in advance by bringing on extra help, whether full time or on a part-time basis. That way, you won't be losing any new business.

Words of caution... ensure that you can handle any extra work with the same commitment to your brand that you did before. Train temporary or part-time employees the same as you do for full-time ones. If not, it's better to pass on new business than to risk your brand reputation.

DON'T bring your bad mood to work and spread it around like a virus.

Bad idea! Sure, we're all human. We have bad days, go through crises, suffer from constipation or colds, and have arguments with our significant others. But if you or employees can't check your problems at the door, you're not going to do the business any justice.

Suck it up! Pretend you're about to perform on stage for an audience. The show must go on. Just try to relax and be authentic and don't force a smile as if you went to bed with a hanger in your mouth!

DON'T make promises to customers and then forget about them.

Have you heard the phrase, "Underpromise and overdeliver?" This philosophy is at the core of exceptional customer service and part of any positive brand experience.

Want to know how to blow your customers away? Tell them you'll deliver or send something on Wednesday, and then on Monday, advise them that it's ready early!

Here's another... when a product has been backordered, substitute an upgraded item and ask the customer if he wants it at the same price.

Whatever you do, don't make promises your company can't keep. This can erode any credibility it may have earned.

DON'T say no to customers or make habitual excuses.

Before you rush to say that a particular product is out of stock or you can't help because it's against company policy, stop and think. Offer to investigate for customers and get back to them.

Sometimes, all it takes is asking a coworker or the business owner to discover that you can serve the customer's needs or request. Smart business people figure out ways to serve customers' needs, even if it means taking a sidestep or two.

Example:

A do-it-yourself homeowner calls a plumbing supplier to see if a specific pipe is in stock. The employee who answers the phone is a community college student working part-time at his uncle's small business. He has received very little training in customer relations and his first response after checking the inventory is, "Sorry, we're out of stock." End of call.

Had the student received some customer service training and really understood the value of a customer and the importance of the brand experience, he would have replied, "We don't have it on stock now, but let me check how quickly I can get one here for you. When do you need it?"

This improved response may not always save a sale, but it's customer centric and demonstrates a willingness to help.

Inevitably, there will be times when you really can't help. By suggesting another supplier or service provider, you show your desire to solve customers' problems and serve their needs. They may remember how helpful you were, and the next time they have a need or problem, will call or visit again.

DON'T be pushy and aggressive with customers.

The last thing you want to do is scare customers away with aggressive behavior or pushy sales techniques. Whether your customers are on the telephone, present in person, or online, your role is to listen and allow them to take the lead.

Never push products or services on customers. Many will shrink back, get annoyed, or leave. Ask questions and listen to them.

When customers are physically present, as in a retail situation, try to gauge and anticipate when they need or want assistance. If you're unsure, ask them nicely, then back off if they say they are simply browsing.

You can do the same thing with other B2C company types, as well as for B2Bs. Try to read customers' body language, tone of voice, or written words to know when to jump in.

There are downsides to being too pushy. Let's say you made a sale, but the customer then experiences buyer's remorse. If you sold her a product, she may return the item, which wasted the time you spent assisting her. If you sold her a service, she may ask or demand that you redo it or refund her money, possibly creating a loss situation for your business.

Another example is when a customer makes a purchase, regrets it, and then badmouths your pushy sales tactics to others. A similar case happened to me while I was vacationing in Key West, Florida.

My husband and I were dallying along Duval Street, when a saleswoman approached me on the sidewalk. She handed me a sample of her store's moisturizing cream and said all the right words to draw me in. Of course, like most women in my age group, I am vulnerable to promises of reduced wrinkles, smoother skin, and younger looks. What gullible dopes we are!

Even though I knew exactly what she was doing, I entered the store regardless. The interior was luxurious and the brand's products beautifully packaged and displayed. The store manager proceeded to wow me with product demonstrations, and I must say, I did see some skin improvement at the time.

After 90 minutes, I walked out a few hundred dollars poorer. Did I really believe that these products would make a difference? Who knows, but my purchase made me feel good temporarily.

When I returned home, I suffered buyer's remorse. I was disappointed that I got suckered in and spent more money than I ever would if I weren't on vacation.

When I checked a couple of online review sites, I read many accounts from disgruntled customers who also felt that they succumbed to overly pushy sales tactics. Would I ever buy this brand again? Heck, no. And I'll advise my friends to be wary of the brand.

DON'T give customers explanations and internal details.

Customers don't give a hoot about your business' internal workings and operations. Why would they?

One time, a cable company representative began to explain why she couldn't accommodate my request. She presented a diatribe on the company's internal protocols and ways of doing business that she thought would justify her situation so I would empathize with her. But guess what? I couldn't care less! And, neither will your customers. Either tell them you'll check into an issue and get back to them, bend over backwards to accommodate them and retain their patronage, or tell them that you can't accommodate their request.

So how can you do things right? Transform your business mindset.

20 WAYS TO TRANSFORM YOUR BUSINESS TO A CUSTOMER-CENTRIC MINDSET

Many recommendations on this list will be familiar to you. As you read through them, you'll probably think that they aren't "rocket science." Admittedly, they're not.

However, there's a big difference between reading them and acknowledging their importance on one hand, and implementing them with authenticity. Any business can tell its employees to do these things, but rote behavior is not the answer. These characteristics need to become second nature to you and your employees if you want your business to transform to a customer-centric mindset.

1. KNOW AND UNDERSTAND YOUR CUSTOMERS

Learn more about your customers — not by being snoopy, but by being friendly. Listen to them, their personal stories, desires, preferences, and complaints. Collect and record important information in your company's customer relationship management program, database, or other customer software for reference. This allows you to anticipate their needs and surprise them.

For the customers you want to target or learn more about, do some online research. In the B2B world, check decision makers' LinkedIn profiles, which are excellent places to uncover their backgrounds, previous employment, skills, and connections.

See if you have anything in common that can open a dialog, prove useful in relationship building, or help you serve them better. Record pertinent information. LinkedIn is one of the best, free prospect and customer research tools around.

For B2C companies, repeat customer purchases can vary greatly. For example, a painting company may have a customer repeat a purchase every five to ten years, whereas an insurance broker's customer is likelier to repeat every six months or a year before a policy expires. On the other hand, a take-out lunch shop in a commercial area may see regular customers every weekday or a few times a week.

Small businesses with frequently repeating customers can learn quite a bit by using online survey tools to conduct brief quantitative surveys. (Quantitative research deals in numbers and statistics.) It's important to capture their e-mail addresses beforehand by using an enticement like entering a draw for a free product or service.

Don't overwhelm customers with too many questions or few people will participate. Use incentives such as electronic gift cards and product coupon codes that produce better response rates and won't incur mailing costs. You don't want to offer costly rewards as these can influence responses. If you can't afford to reward each survey participant, create a lottery in which each participant is eligible to win one higher-value prize.

For businesses whose customers repeat infrequently or are conceivably one time only, you'll want to learn more about them as a group. During transactions, observe and make notes to help you understand them. Perhaps you want to know who your ideal customers are by demographics: age, educational level, economic status, type of employment, and race. What you can't observe, you can ask, indicating that you're doing marketing research for your company. If yours is a neighborhood business, there's a wealth of information by zip code at the US Census Bureau or by geographic area in Canada at Statistics Canada.

When you want to know more about individuals, check social media sites to see what they've shared and posted. Depending on what type of information you're seeking, it's amazing what people share online. Then see if they have any profiles on review sites like Yelp, MerchantCircle, or Google to learn about their preferences and expectations of other vendors.

Make the documented information easy for everyone in the business to access. It does take time to enter the information the first time, but once you establish a system, adding to it regularly will be quicker. Moreover, the benefits of having your customer data at your fingertips will outweigh the initial data entry time. The more you know about your customers, the more you can personalize your company's services to dazzle them.

2. BE HONEST AND FORTHRIGHT

You can't earn customers' trust if you lie, stretch the truth, or gloss over problems. When you're open and honest with them, they'll respect you. You'll begin to gain their confidence.

When a salesperson tells me not to purchase a particular item because I won't like it (for whatever reason), I admire that. I assume that her candor has saved me some aggravation or discontent and I'm always grateful.

Example:

I visited a neighborhood pool supply store to replace our skimmer. (Remember, I live in Arizona — pools are heaven when it's 108° F/42° C.) It was my first time in the store and I was unfamiliar with pool products.

The salesman told me that my broken skimmer was a low-end product and replacing it with a similar unit would produce the same results. He showed me different varieties from $12.99 up to those approaching $100. I was unsure which would be best at a reasonable price point.

When I pointed out a product he hadn't shown me, asking if it would serve my needs, he said it wouldn't and explained why. Aha! That built up my level of trust for this guy. Before that, I wasn't sure. So I purchased the skimmer that he recommended, hich also happened to be on sale. Bonus.

If I had discovered that he wasn't genuine with me, it

would have been the end of my patronage. I wouldn't have gone back — ever. It's not as if that store is the only pool vendor in my area. There are many in a warm climate like mine.

3. LISTEN, LISTEN, AND LISTEN AGAIN

Customers are the best information source on your company's brand. Knowing what they like and dislike about its products and services will help your business identify its strengths and weaknesses in the marketplace. Customer input can also help ascertain any new opportunities your business may not have previously recognized and can guide any changes for improvement.

Unlike corporations, small businesses do not always have the budgets needed to conduct thorough marketing research. However, there are less costly methods to help you gain an understanding of your customers' feedback.

Use online surveys as I described previously. If you aren't experienced in developing unbiased survey questions, review some professionally developed customer satisfaction questionnaires to learn how to frame your questions. There is a science to writing survey questions so they don't skew results. If you have the funds, hire a marketing consultant or researcher to assist with the project and ensure that you include incentives and/or rewards for respondent participation.

Use the old-fashioned telephone and call a cross section of customers. Ask them the same series of open-ended (qualitative) questions and take notes of their responses. Don't forget to send them a token of your appreciation for participating.

For B2B companies, take individual customers to lunch and elicit their feedback. If you have good relationships, ask them for their candid input and take notes.

For B2C, an informal way to elicit feedback is to ask customers at the point of sale. Whether this occurs at a checkout desk, a customer's home, on the telephone, or online, the brand experience is fresh in their minds.

Not everyone will feel 100% comfortable telling you the truth, especially if you are standing right there. Do you tell the restaurant manager the truth when she asks how your meal was?

What if she explains why she's asking for your honest feedback and that she welcomes it? Would you feel more inclined to share it? The advantage to this approach is having the opportunity to fix issues when customers share their negative experiences at the moment. Don't let the transaction end without making every effort to resolve any concerns they express.

Another excellent source of feedback, especially for B2B, involves the prospects who chose not to become customers. When following up with them after providing a quote or estimate, and they indicate that they selected another supplier, you have nothing to lose by asking which factors contributed to eliminating your company. Encourage their honesty by mentioning that you want to learn how to do better next time. They may not always comply but it's worth a shot.

Listening Tip:

When dealing with customers in any communication channel, make sure you don't interrupt them, especially when they're complaining. Listen attentively until they finish, be empathetic, ask questions for clarification, and then respond.

Genuinely show interest in what customers have to say at every point during the sales cycle. Listen while keeping eye contact and smile whenever you're in the same physical location. Smile even when you're on the telephone with them as studies show that telephone smiling can positively affect outcomes.

Acquiring data from your customers is just the first step. Analyzing it with a cross-section of company managers and employees, then brainstorming on ways you can plug the gaps, improve processes, take advantage of new opportunities, and fix whatever is broken, will take it further. This is also a wonderful time to celebrate what is working and reward the team for their efforts.

4. LOSE THE SILO MENTALITY

If you are a solopreneur, feel free to skip this part.

No matter how many employees your small business may have, it's important to foster a culture of cohesion, collaboration, internal communication, and teamwork. Maintaining silos of competing departments and egos can be extremely detrimental to your business.

Remember that customers don't care about your company's internal structure. The last thing they want to hear is "That's not my job," or "That's not my department," or "Sorry, I can't help you."

Nurturing a customer-centric philosophy can contribute to a more collaborative team and better external service. Ensure employees are aware of company policies, whether or not these affect their areas of responsibility. Especially in a small business, employees must be prepared to fill in for coworkers or handle customers' problems, even when they are unfamiliar with the customer or the situation.

Breaking down barriers will help create a more holistic work environment, which in turn will have a positive effect on external customer relations. Customer centrism can greatly reduce employee finger pointing, blaming, and appearing disjointed and dysfunctional.

5. COMMUNICATE WITH CUSTOMERS

Communicating regularly with customers is essential for customer engagement, building brand loyalty, and getting more word-of-mouth referrals.

During the sales and fulfillment stage:

For B2B and nonretail B2C companies, it's imperative to keep customers up to date on their orders or projects. You can accomplish this by using customer communication management programs or Software-as-a-Service (SaaS). Admittedly, this is not my area of expertise, so I recommend seeking assistance if you want to explore a technology solution.

For small businesses that don't need software solutions, the old-fashioned telephone and e-mail work just fine. Here's an example from my own small business:

Every time customers place a custom printing or promotional product order, my husband e-mails them updates. First, he thanks them for their orders and advises them of the estimated shipping date. Once he receives notification that the orders have been shipped, he e-mails again, advising customers of their expected delivery dates.

Sure, this takes extra time but this type of personalized communication and service is why customers patronize small businesses.

The 2014 *Small Business Saturday Consumer Insights Survey* underscored this point. Nearly all (94%) of US consumers say that "shopping at small businesses makes them 'feel good'" and more than half (57%) say they know one or more of their local small business owners personally.

You can capitalize on this personal touch when there are delays or changes in customers' orders or projects.

Communicate with them immediately and don't wait until they become impatient or annoyed that a deadline has passed. They'll appreciate your proactive approach.

When making promises, it's better to err on the side of caution than to disappoint customers. Add some extra time to your estimates in case unforeseen circumstances happen that are beyond your control. Then when things finish on time, your customers will be thrilled that you met their expectations early.

Follow up with them. During and after completing an order or project, contact them to ask if everything is alright and if there's anything further you can do for them.

On a regular basis:

Communicating with customers regularly is important if you want to build relationships, maintain engagement, and sustain or grow your business. Reach out to them in friendship.

Every great business is built on friendship.
(JC Penney)

There are many ways to achieve this goal.

Content Marketing

Although content marketing has existed for eons, now it has a dedicated name and strong position in the marketing mix. It helps solve the problem that Jay Baer described in his book, *Youtility: Why Smart Marketing Is about Help Not Hype*:

You can't promote to people you can't find.

Content marketing is a strategy that helps broaden your company's audiences and brand by supplying free, relevant content that demonstrates expertise and knowledge in order to acquire, retain, and engage customers. Using a variety of marketing communications vehicles such as newsletters, direct mail, e-mails, websites, publications, blogs, videos, and social media, you can liberally offer advice and guidance to customers without overtly pitching and promoting your business.

The *Kentico 2014 Content Marketing Survey* found that 74% of the general public trusts content from businesses that aim to educate readers about a particular topic. But, "even signing off an otherwise objective blog post or newsletter with a product pitch will bring the content's credibility level down by 29%."

You can also host webinars, video conferences, or virtual trade shows to educate target audiences in your area of expertise. The more they learn and know, the better they will understand and appreciate your recommendations, products, and/or services.

By placing customers at the center of every communication, you can focus on content that they will find relevant and valuable. Share customer stories, offer information about your field of specialization, and help them solve problems.

Content marketing gives your small business an opportunity to build a network of followers and brand believers. The more that prospects and customers perceive your business as an expert and a leader in its field, the more attractive it becomes when they need its products and/or services.

Additionally, as your network builds, people will share your content with others. The higher the sharing volume, the greater the chances of getting in front of prospects who happen to need your products and services at that moment.

One thing to keep in mind, however, is that Facebook and Twitter have become so saturated that reaching your audiences organically is nearly impossible to accomplish without buying display ads.

Countless examples of content marketing are thriving online. For starters, you can search for blog posts on your business' main topics at Google Blog Search, explore professional or industry-related LinkedIn groups, and check out SlideShare for presentations.

Excellent resources on content marketing are also available, such as:

- Content Marketing Institute (http://contentmarketinginstitute.com)

- *Content Rules: How to Create Killer Blogs, Podcasts, Videos, Ebooks, Webinars (and More) That Engage Customers and Ignite Your Business* by Ann Handley and C.C. Chapman

- *The New Rules of Marketing & PR: How to Use Social Media, Online Video, Mobile Applications, Blogs, News Releases, and Viral Marketing to Reach Buyers Directly* by David Meerman Scott

- *Epic Content Marketing: How to Tell a Different Story, Break through the Clutter, and Win More Customers by Marketing Less* by Joe Pulizzi

At this point, you may be wondering why you should give away your expertise for free when you're trying to acquire paying customers. It is a very good question — one that I asked, too, when I first focused on content marketing.

Oddly enough, content marketing does not replace the demand for your company's products and services. It actually enriches it. While your business offers advice, information, and education, it can increase web traffic (attracting more leads), boost search engine optimization (SEO), and get in front of more prospects when people share its content.

Social Media

You can communicate with individual customers and groups by using social media. Send personalized direct messages to individuals using Twitter, Facebook, or LinkedIn, such as blog post and article links that relate to their businesses, industries, or professions.

When you want to send messages to a wider audience, you can use the company's Facebook page and LinkedIn messaging. Or invite customers to join your online communities on Facebook, LinkedIn, or Google+. Social media gives you the opportunity to connect with, and engage, customers outside of content marketing or as part of a content marketing strategy.

E-Mails

I will go against the flow of some marketers who claim that e-mail marketing is dead. Of course, there are pluses and minuses to every communication channel, but e-mail is still a common and effective form of business communication.

You can communicate with individual customers quickly and efficiently by using your business e-mail address. From a risk management perspective, it gives you a record of what both parties said. And it takes so little time to send messages – way faster than picking up the telephone.

When communicating with groups, you can't beat using an e-mail service provider (ESP). It is affordable, provides the necessary tools and templates, measures your efforts, and helps build your audiences.

Outside of content marketing, you can use ESPs to advise customers of your holiday hours or weather closings; promote sales, new products or services; and send greetings. However, there are a few downsides to group e-mail communications.

Spam filters can make it challenging to get through to some inboxes. Using triggers like "100% free" or symbols like "!" or "$" in your subject line can actually block your messages.

If your company's database is large, monthly ESP fees can be costly. Also, because people receive so many promotional e-mails today, average open and click-through rates are low.

The best advice I can offer is to test this communication channel and gauge your success. The advantages may outweigh the disadvantages.

Postcards

Postcards are probably one of the most underrated forms of business communication. Yet they can get attention in ways that digital communications cannot.

When I first started my business, I developed branded company postcards to use for individual communication such as thanking customers for their recent business. They're also excellent for acknowledging special milestones such as business anniversaries or personal accomplishments and sending new networking colleagues a short note saying how nice it was to meet them.

Customer Research

You can communicate regularly with customers and ask for feedback on any variety of issues – both individually and collectively. Solicit their opinions on your marketing communications collateral, new products or services you are considering, or what their own experiences have been on a specific topic.

Approach this in a warm and personal way, telling customers that you value their opinions. This sends a strong message of appreciation as well.

Research and learn about your customers' personal lives and interests to reveal the things you share in common so you can communicate with and engage them. This is where small businesses frequently have an advantage over corporations.

6. RESPOND TO CUSTOMERS QUICKLY

We can all relate to being on the other end of this issue. Ask yourself how many times you lost your patience or got aggravated with a business that did not respond quickly enough to you. Probably more than you care to remember, right?

Don't lose sight of those personal experiences when you are dealing with your customers. Treat them as you would want to be treated.

The quicker you can respond to an inquiry or resolve an issue, the less chance there is of forgetting about it or letting it slide down your 'to-do' list. We've all been there — frantically writing notes on a piece of scratch paper as we listen to customers.

How many of these pieces of paper remain on your desk at the end of the day? The end of the week? How many times have you discovered misplaced pieces of paper to which you never responded?

Using technology for this purpose, such as Evernote, Microsoft OneNote, or mobile note-taking apps, can help mitigate the problem. For those who still prefer taking notes, the sooner you complete the task, the less anxiety you will have wondering which customers you forgot. Customers will appreciate your quick reply. In fact, the sooner you get back to them, the more you can 'wow' them.

One time, when I called my father's doctor on his behalf, the medical assistant told me that she wouldn't have a chance to consult with the doctor until the end of the day, after which she would call me back with the answer to my question. Imagine my surprise when she did so 10 minutes later! These kinds of positive customer interactions contribute to customer and brand loyalty.

7. MAINTAIN A POSITIVE ATTITUDE

I'll bet you've heard this advice limitless times. The weird thing is that as much as people know this, they don't always follow it! Yet maintaining a positive attitude at work can make a big difference in your customers' brand experiences.

If you (or employees) come to work edgy, grumpy, or unhappy, it will surely come through to your internal and external customers. You may think you're demonstrating a positive attitude, but your voice inflections and body language may say something else altogether.

Some human resource professionals and personnel psychologists claim that your mindset at work can play a major role in attracting, retaining, and engaging with customers, connecting with coworkers, getting a raise or promotion, and achieving your personal career goals.

Of all the soft skills most valued by employers, having a positive attitude comes in at number one (36%) according to the *2014 Canadian Education and Research Institute for Counselling National Business Survey*.

Canadian businessman, Isadore Sharp, founder and chairman of Four Seasons Hotels and Resorts and author of *Four Seasons – The Story of a Business Philosophy* (2009), summed this up well:

We want people who like other people, and are therefore more motivated to serve them. Competence we can teach; attitude is ingrained.

How true is that?

8. BE FRIENDLY AND PERSONABLE

Most customers and prospects like to deal with friendly, nice people who can answer their questions, handle their complaints or issues, demonstrate humility, empathize with them, be patient, and relate to them as human beings. Being friendly to both internal and external customers is everyone's responsibility in your business.

A Kingston University Business School in London 2013 study revealed that a simple smile and a friendly greeting can make customers feel much more loyal towards small independent companies. Unfortunately, just over half those sampled stated their small business employed this practice.

Smiling and friendliness don't cost anything!

Check out this YouTube video from author and speaker Jeffrey Gitomer. It says it all.

http://youtu.be/LPzMEiw5XyM.

(Ensure that "Safety Mode" is off.)

9. DEMONSTRATE FLEXIBILITY

Flexibility is one area where small businesses can outshine the larger ones. Being smaller gives your company the ability to bend and adapt as needed.

With fewer people (or just one person), there are fewer bosses to approve a customer service decision. Ideally, your employees have been empowered to make flexible decisions without the need to ask someone else.

Flexibility is a major key to providing amazing service. Whenever possible, try saying, "yes" to customers before instinctively replying, "It's not our policy," or "Sorry, I can't do that," or "That's not how we do things."

Have you ever seen the 1970 film *Five Easy Pieces* with Jack Nicholson and Karen Black? It has a diner scene where Nicholson's character (Robert Duprea) wants to order an omelet and toast, but there's no toast on the menu. The server does not budge on the "no substitutions" policy and Duprea grows more frustrated and angry.

"I don't make the rules," says the waitress.

To watch the clip of this poor customer service example of inflexibility, visit YouTube and keyword search "Five Easy Pieces" and look for "diner scene." Wait for the scene ending. It is *not* pretty.

There is one important limitation to flexibility that requires alternative solutions. You wouldn't want to make any decisions that could damage your business brand in the long run.

Losing a few bucks to retain a valuable customer might be a necessity, but taking a big financial hit or disregarding your other customers would not be in your business' best interest. In other words, use your discretion.

10. BE PROACTIVE AND ANTICIPATE NEEDS

Small businesses have an advantage over larger companies in this area, too. There are typically fewer customers to know and track than at larger companies, making it easier to anticipate their needs.

Some B2C companies have the ability to impress regular customers when they arrive on location. An example is a coffee shop employee who knows her 'regulars' and their preferences. As these customers enter, she starts making their preferred coffees. Now these are impressive brand experiences!

Watch customers' behaviors and body language wherever you deliver your products or services – at their homes or offices, in their stores, or other locales. Note what they tell you about their preferences and needs and act upon them.

For B2B (and B2C) businesses, customer relationship management (CRM) and inventory or sales management software can facilitate tracking and analyzing customer service: customers' purchases, preferences, and loyalty program participation, in addition to sales, marketing, and technical support histories.

However, be aware that 75% of CRM initiatives fail to substantially impact the customer experience, according to an article by Preact CRM in the *CRM SoftwareBlog*. And, why? Because they lacked an effective implementation strategy.

If you're prepared to develop a proper CRM strategy, it's worth exploring CRM options or improving on the system you currently have. Some free and inexpensive CRM programs include: Batchbook, CRM.me, Free CRM, Infusionsoft, Pipedrive, and Zoho CRM.

Being proactive means not only anticipating customer needs, but also helping them avoid unwanted problems or added costs of which they may not even be aware. When I discover that a customer is using his business e-mail account to send hundreds of communications, I always advise him of the risks. Although it has no cost, as compared with using an e-mail service provider (ESP), he can unwittingly be in violation of the CAN-SPAM Act, rules established by the Federal Trade Commission (FTC) in the US (other countries have similar legislation).

His e-mail address may also get blocked by many ESPs so his communication may never reach some of his intended recipients. Most small business people I advise had no idea of these repercussions and appreciate my advice. Being proactive and helping customers avoid problems like this are part of being customer centric and building their trust in your business.

Following up with customers is another aspect of being on the ball. It is also connected to #5 – communicating with customers, #6 – responding to customers quickly, and #17 – taking responsibility. One of the biggest complaints customers make is when companies do not follow up with them.

No one wants to chase you to buy your products or services. Usually, many competitors are willing to serve your customers better, speedier, and more consistently.

11. BE SINCERE, RESPECTFUL, AND HUMAN

As we learned earlier in this chapter, many customers don't like "canned" or "scripted" responses. If business owners (or employees) manage customers in a rote manner, their insincerity will give them away.

Use customers' names when you talk with them. It can really help personalize the conversation and show your interest in them as people. If they call on the telephone, ask for their names and write them down. Then try using their names two to three times in your conversation, depending on its length. If your communication is by e-mail, you can use their names at least once in your content.

Don't be reticent to have a personal chat with customers. The few minutes it takes for friendly chatter is an investment in bonding the relationship.

Years ago, I remember hearing a small business owner criticize one of his employees for talking too much with customers. He was concerned that she couldn't get her "work" done.

Well a funny thing happened. The employee had such wonderful relationships with customers, that when she left for another job, the company lost several of its customers! Now imagine if everyone in the company dealt with customers in the same manner? It may not have lost any customers!

It's amazing what you can find in common with your customers. It can be a shared passion for a specific sport or pastime, a place to which you've both traveled, or something in the news. When you can't find anything else, the weather is always good fodder for a quick conversation that seems to find common ground.

Treat your customers with the same respect and warmth as you do to your friends, neighbors, and colleagues. Just remember to avoid topics like religion and politics, both of which can turn unfriendly quickly!

12. TURN COMPLAINTS INTO CONTENTMENT

Some business people perceive customer complaints as a pain in the butt. I suggest they take a 180° turn on this attitude.

Customer complaints are *gifts* to your business. (Yes, you read that right.) Although the majority of customers will not take the time to voice their discontent, the ones who do can give you opportunities to investigate and identify where internal problems lie. The rest simply won't come back and you won't know why.

9 Steps in Managing Customer Complaints

#1. When customers complain, first, listen attentively and do not interrupt. If customers are in front of you, establish eye contact, lean in, and genuinely show interest. You can occasionally nod your head or say something brief to encourage them to continue their stories.

If customers use e-mails or online chat to complain, use your judgment. If complaints are lengthy or more detailed, you're better off asking if you can contact them on the telephone to assist them.

#2. After they finish, thank them for bringing the matter to your attention. How else would you learn of these issues?

#3. Apologize for the error, misunderstanding, or whatever the concern is — even if you don't agree with it. Say something like, "I'm so sorry that happened," without pointing fingers of blame or repeating the entire issue.

#4. Clarify their stories by summarizing them in your own words. You can say, "I've taken some notes and want to check if I've gotten everything right." This gives you the opportunity to ensure you've noted all the facts, plus it validates what customers have said. Ask questions when you're unsure of something or need to fill any gaps.

#5. Demonstrate your empathy. Say things like, "I can see why that has upset you" or "That must have frustrated you."

#6. Remember that customers prefer instant resolutions. If an investigation is required before taking the next step, advise them that you'll get back to them and when. Then follow up.

If no investigation is necessary, ask customers how you can make things right for them. Sometimes, all they want is recognition of the problem and/or an apology. In these cases, I recommend that you send token physical or electronic gifts, acknowledging your appreciation for their valuable feedback.

When customers ask for something tangible, like a discount, a refund, a credit for next time, or a free product, make sure you empower employees to give customers what they've asked for – if requests are reasonable. If not, offer predetermined alternatives. (Predetermined giveaways are offers that you can suggest immediately to customers so manager approval is unnecessary.)

I recommend asking customers what they want first before offering anything else. Years ago, when filing a complaint with my former cell phone provider, the customer service representative apologized and said that she added 60 minutes of extra national talk time to my account. I told her how much I appreciated the gesture, but since I had just moved to the US from Canada, I knew few people in the States to call! Her gesture had zero value to me.

When attempting to retain complaining customers, make sure that "make-up" gifts or offers have value to them. Your automatic offers may not have the same worth to your customers as you think they will.

#7. Tell customers what you plan to do – and DO IT promptly!

#8. Follow up after the situation has been resolved. Make a quick telephone call whenever possible; it will be more personal than sending an e-mail or using another communication method.

#9. Learn from these experiences and prevent future mistakes.

Following these 9 steps can convert complaining customers into content and loyal ones.

13. BE CONSISTENT

Although I discussed consistent messaging and communications in Idea #1, consistency also applies to customer-centric service and engagement. Like all other brand touchpoints, your business' actions should be equally consistent as its words and messages.

Customers remain loyal to companies that provide the same brand experiences with every interaction. They have expectations that the products, services, and experiences they had previously will be the same the next time and after that. When your business has proven itself to customers consistently, that's when word-of-mouth (WOM) referrals and positive reviews take off.

Here's an example of why consistency is so important: My sister and father tried a new deli in town and were very impressed with its food and service. So much so, that my sister purchased Groupons for two more visits.

Unfortunately, the next time they went for dinner, the food was lackluster and they regretted buying the third Groupon. They used up their final voucher but the food did not improve. Their initial excitement at discovering a good local deli soon fizzled quickly.

As a start-up in a very competitive market, the deli couldn't afford to lose any new customers. With its success resting on WOM referrals from friends, family, and neighbors, its future certainly looked grim. Eventually, it closed its doors.

To avoid this type of situation, ensure that your business products, services, processes, and standards align with a customer-centric philosophy. All employees should be responsible for consistent product and service quality, behavior, and engagement.

14. GO THE EXTRA MILE

Research shows that consumers prefer small businesses to larger ones when it comes to service. As I pointed out earlier, there's satisfactory service, and then there's exceptional service.

People remember exceptional service and can retell amazing customer service stories years after they happened. That's how memorable they can be.

Some great examples:

In preparation for submitting a bid to a client, a kitchen designer looked through the family's existing kitchen drawers and storage and took photos of all the contents. No, she wasn't being purposefully nosy. She wanted to ensure that her bid was based on accommodating everything the family currently had in their kitchen. Now that's impressive!

A few years back, while staying in La Jolla, California for a speaking engagement, I grabbed a taxi from town to my hotel. In the course of the conversation, the driver learned that I had never been to that area before.

When he offered to show me some sites, I was a bit reticent, thinking he was either a serial killer or simply vying for a big fare. But when he added that there wouldn't be an extra charge, I was flabbergasted.

He drove me to the mountain top to see the beautiful homes and vista before dropping me off at the hotel safely. That's going the extra mile — literally!

One important thing to clarify. Customer centricity does not mean "giving away the store" to exceed expectations and wow a customer. Self-preservation must trump fulfilling customers' needs if the cost is too high. Sometimes, it means letting a customer go, ideally on good terms.

15.KEEP PROMISES

Keeping promises in life is important to our credibility as people. No one likes to associate with friends or relatives who are like the father Jim Carrey played in the film *Liar Liar*. He starts the movie as an outright liar who makes promises to his son that he never keeps.

It's similar for small businesses. Your company's promises represent its word and brand reputation. When your company cannot keep its promises, it can have more of a detrimental effect to the bottom line than it can in larger companies.

First, the business has fewer customers to manage, and second, those customers may be more closely aligned through WOM referrals. Break a promise to a customer and a network of friends and family may hear about it.

Here are examples of the wrong and right ways to manage promises:

You take your car in for repairs and the mechanic says it will be ready by 3:00 p.m. You call at 3:00 and he says it's not ready; check again in half an hour. You call again and the same thing happens. You finally retrieve your car at 6:05 p.m. Grrr.

Versus:

You take your car in for repairs and the mechanic says it will be ready by 3:00 p.m. At 2:00, he calls and says your car is ready for pickup. You show up, pay the bill, and he thanks you for your business as he hands you a $5 discount coupon for your next visit. Now that's underpromising and overdelivering at its best!

16. FOSTER DIVERSITY

Your customers may have many similarities and differences. If your business is located in one geographic area, chances are greater that your customers will share similar demographics — age, income, education, etc., but their psychographics (attitudes, beliefs, and tastes) may vary.

Over the past few years, diversity has been a major focus for many corporations and larger companies. Employees and customers with diverse backgrounds, races, ethnicities, and cultures, in addition to age and gender differences, have brought unique talents and experiences to both their workplaces and the marketplace.

High-performing organizations recognize that the aim of diversity is not just meeting compliance targets, but tapping into the diverse perspectives and approaches each individual employee brings to the workplace. Moving beyond diversity to focus on inclusion as well requires companies to examine how fully the organization embraces new ideas, accommodates different styles of thinking,... creates a more flexible work environment, enables people to connect and collaborate, and encourages different types of leaders. ("Global Human Capital Trends 2014: Engaging the 21st-century workforce," Deloitte Consulting LLP)

By committing to diversity as a strategic imperative, companies align their own organisation more closely with an increasingly heterogeneous customer base. This enables them to forge stronger bonds with customers in two respects: reaching key purchasing decision makers and taking a customer perspective. (Vivian Hunt, Dennis Layton, Sara Prince, "Diversity Matters," McKinsey & Company)

Businesses that support diversity, inside and out, foster an attitude of openness and equality, both of which contribute to a customer-centric brand reputation.

One special group of diverse employees and customers comprises people with disabilities. Having previously worked for an organization that served the physical disability community, I oversaw the marketing of sensitivity and awareness training programs to corporations. I would highly recommend it for every business, irrespective of size.

I encourage your company to hire people with disabilities. There are many proven advantages, all of which can contribute to your company's brand reputation. You can reduce hiring and training costs, attract a wider customer base, increase retention, improve employee morale, and boost profits. Plus, some states and provinces offer tax incentives and cover the costs of necessary accommodations.

As for the business case in serving this population, people with physical, mental, and sensory disabilities are the third largest market in the US. At 54 million strong, they surpass Hispanics, African Americans, and Asian Americans, as well as Generation X and teens.

In Canada, about 3.8 million people, or 13.7% of Canadians aged 15 and older, reported being limited in their daily activities because of disabilities. If we add family members, friends, and associates, people with disabilities represent a trillion dollars in purchasing power!

For more on this, visit Think Beyond the Label in the US or the Council of Canadians with Disabilities in Canada.

17. TAKE RESPONSIBILITY

When it comes to determining who is responsible for the customer centrism of your brand, there is no doubt. Everyone internally must share this responsibility.

Providing exceptional internal and external customer service should be priority number one in employees' job descriptions. When you're in hiring mode, look for the 'right' people who won't shy away from taking initiative and responsibility, no matter what their positions or titles are.

Try this exercise with your existing employees:

Assign a small team to identify every customer brand touchpoint for each market segment. Begin with customer entry points through purchase and fulfillment.

Once you have a flowchart or list of experiences in the "customer journey," record which employees are responsible for these touchpoints. If you identify any gaps, plug them.

The next step is to ensure that each employee has a copy of the customer journey map and understands it. They need to know customer touchpoints, which people are responsible for them, what their job functions are, and how they interact with customers and/or suppliers. Having this knowledge gives employees the tools to take responsibility whenever required.

One way to accomplish this is to ask employees to make individual or group presentations to the rest of the team during a meeting or company lunch. They can describe which customer journey touchpoints they have responsibility for and other employees can ask questions for clarification.

Not only does this enhance employees' general knowledge, it also engages them and makes the learning process fun. By going through this exercise, employees can gain confidence in managing customer relations and being accountable, even when a situation doesn't fall within their areas of expertise. They may not necessarily be able to replace their coworkers, but they can certainly improve their customer management skills rather than passing the buck and possibly losing customers.

Another form of taking responsibility is when employees respond to customers' inbound communications. Let's say Jim is working while the rest of the staff are are out for lunch. The phone rings and he knows he's responsible for answering.

Connie Chan, a regular customer, asks Jim if she can can add to an order she had placed earlier that day. Rather than asking her to call back when the sales representative is back in the office or sending her to voicemail, Jim listens and takes notes.

He has a friendly conversation with Ms. Chan and advises her that he will pass the information on to Mario (her sales representative). He assures her that Mario will e-mail her to confirm the additional order when he returns.

Once Mario is back in the office, Jim shares the information. But Jim's responsibility does not end there. He asks Mario to e-mail Ms. Chan to confirm the order, with a copy (cc) to him. This way, Jim can keep tabs on the customer request until Mario follows up, enabling him to fulfill his responsibility.

When you create a work environment where everyone covers everyone else's backs, and the customer is at the center of it all, your team will recognize this type of interaction between Jim and Mario as helpful and collaborative.

18. SHOW APPRECIATION

Showing appreciation to your customers, employees, suppliers, and others who contribute to your small business operations is imperative in maintaining successful relationships. Creating happiness and positive feelings can be contagious. Demonstrating authentic concern for people and patting them on the back when appropriate are so simple and cost so little to do.

Employee Appreciation

If you are a solopreneur, feel free to skip this part.

According to the *2014 TINYpulse Employee Engagement and Organizational Culture Report:*

Organizations are underperforming when it comes to showing how valued employees are, with only 21% of employees saying they feel strongly valued. Lack of appreciation and recognition is driving employees to feel undervalued. Given the premium Millennials put on feeling valued, this metric will only get worse.

There are several ways in which your small business can show its appreciation to employees. One option is to use an employee recognition program or platform that gives your business the tools and means to recognize employees. A 2013 study conducted by the Society of Human Resource Management (SHRM)/Globoforce reported an increase in employee recognition programs. One of the study's key findings was that employees were more motivated and performed better when rewarded through both praise and prize.

How you say it matters. So does what you give... Employees don't want to just hear 'good job.' They crave tangible rewards to go along with that praise. (SHRM/Globoforce Employee Recognition Survey, Spring 2013 Report)

The study also noted that recognizing employees for their achievements would make them understand the company's objectives, which would lead to greater alignment with the company's financial goals. So overall, it would be a win-win situation.

Several employee recognition platforms are available online that small businesses may find valuable. In addition to peer and management recognition, some of these platforms incorporate a reward system, peer or customer feedback, company social networking, performance management, culture management, and team communications.

Some of the less costly employee recognition platforms include: Achievers, AwardCo, Bonusly, crewHu, GiveAWow, Kudos, Teamphoria, and YouEarnedIt. If your business is relatively small or an employee recognition platform is not a good fit, then another option is to develop your own employee appreciation program. This can be as simple as keeping track of employees' accomplishments and praising and rewarding them accordingly. Alternatively, you can schedule specific rewards throughout the calendar year.

Here are just a few low-cost ideas to get you started. You can do these separately or combine them, whichever suits your needs.

- Write handwritten thank-you notes.

- Give out gift cards for movies, coffee, restaurants, bookstores, etc.

- Pay tribute to employees, individually or at staff meetings.

- Feature them in company newsletters or on the website.

- Celebrate employees' milestone anniversaries company wide. According to the *Workforce Mood Tracker, Spring 2014 Report*, "Adapting to the Realities of Our Changing Workforce," 73% of respondents preferred that service awards / recognition come from managers and others, not from their managers alone.

- Take them to lunch individually.

- If you have some nice promotional products on hand, give them out as appreciation and recognition gifts. (No, not the 39¢ pen!)

- Give them a half or full day off.

- Buy a birthday cake for each employee's birthday.

- Plan games or theme days at your workplace.

- Plan a potluck lunch with employees supplying food that represent their various cultural backgrounds.

- Create company currency that employees can collect and cash in for privileges like taking a longer lunch break, taking a day off, or coming in late.

Here are some ideas that cost a few bucks but won't break the bank:

- Plan a staff lunch and order pizza or sandwich trays.

- Depending on how many employees there are, take them all out for lunch.

- Plan a fun event for the entire team and if feasible, take the afternoon off for it. Team-building ideas that can work well: bowling, paintball, BBQ, or an indoor/outdoor amusement facility.

- Give them gift certificates for healthy or relaxing experiences like massage therapy, spa services, yoga classes, or gym visits.

- Periodically, bring in healthy treats for the break room or meetings like whole grain bagels, muffins, fruit, nuts, and cereal bars.

- Hire a massage therapist to give employees neck and shoulder massages at their desks.

I recommend that you put together some options and elicit employees' responses or brainstorm with them to create a list. After all, they are your internal customers and it's best to select rewards they will value. The key to success here is to plan these activities so you don't overlook them.

One thing you can do right now is to write this date down on your calendar: March 1, Employee Appreciation Day. Even though employee appreciation should be top of mind throughout the year, this date gives you the opportunity to truly celebrate and plan something special for employees.

One additional note: In some places, employee gifts may be deemed as taxable income. I suggest that you contact your business' tax advisor to learn if there are any tax implications for your employees.

Customer Appreciation

Customers who feel appreciated and valued tend to stick around, increase their purchasing, and recommend your small business to others. As long as your company continues to provide exceptional service and products at price points customers value, they won't have a reason to change suppliers.

There are many customer appreciation and loyalty programs offered from specialty companies and consultants. Some of the online platforms include: Belly, Firefly Rewards, FiveStars, Loyalty Gator, Perka, Perkville, and Pirq.

Aside from your employees demonstrating verbal appreciation to customers after each transaction, occasionally add the element of surprise to truly wow them. Here are some ways your B2C business can demonstrate appreciation to its customers.

- Give out a small gift or promotional product after completed transactions.

- Give out discount coupons for future purchases.

- For customers who make larger purchases, give out gift cards for movies, restaurants, or other products and services. Alternatively, give them bank gift cards so they can use these for whatever they want.

- For retail businesses, use scratch cards or other ways that give customers a chance to win a free purchase or discount on their current purchase.

- Hold customer appreciation sales.

- If you have your customers' e-mail addresses, send them coupons or coupon codes for merchandise or service discounts.

- Develop a simple system where customers accumulate reward points.

- Send them post-purchase thank-you letters hand signed by the business owner, president, or CEO.

Here are some ways your B2B segment can demonstrate appreciation to its customers.

- Depending on how many customers you have, hold a customer appreciation event and invite them to your location for an open house, after-work cocktail reception, or early-morning breakfast.

- Invite customers to hear a speaker on a topic that your company and their businesses have in common.

- Reward customers for business referrals.

- Send promotional product gifts that match how much business they give you. Products are available in every price range.

- Send flowers, edible gift baskets, gift cards with personal notes, or discount coupons for future purchases.

- Showcase a customer in your company newsletter or on the website.

- Send birthday cards.

- Send holiday gifts.

- Mention them in one of your blog or social media posts (with a link to their sites, where applicable).

- Send restaurant gift certificates and tell them that dinner is "on you."

- Send movie gift cards with a note sharing your favorite current films.

- Give them an upgraded product, an extra service, or a special discount.

- Give them a free product or service.

- If they live in the same location, take them to lunch individually.

- Make charitable donations honoring them. Most charities will send them acknowledgments for your gift.

- Sponsor their participation in a conference or business event.

- Next time you're at a conference, send them copies of any relevant handouts.

Again, there are many ideas you can develop to ensure that your customers feel appreciated. Enlist your employees' help for additional ideas. The important thing is consistency.

Develop a customer appreciation strategy that is realistic for your company size and budget. Ensure you assign the tactics in your plan, so one person isn't responsible for overlooking everything. This is a great way to engage and empower your employees.

Feeling appreciated is one of the most important needs that people have. When you share with someone your appreciation and gratitude, they will not forget you. Appreciation will return to you many times. (SearchQuotes.com, "Steve Brunkhorst Quotes & Sayings")

19. ADVISE, DON'T "SELL"

When you advise your customers rather than "sell" to them, you can gain their trust and retain them longer. Offer your unbiased recommendations in your newsletters and other content, as well as in one-to-one conversations.

Ask them questions to determine what they may need to solve a problem, avoid a problem, or make their lives easier. For luxury products and services, when need is not a motivating factor, you can still advise them on the best features and benefits that can serve their wants and lifestyles.

As author Jay Baer wrote in his book, *Youtility*:

If you sell something, you make a customer today. If you help someone, you may create a customer for life.

20. DEVELOP CUSTOMER EXPERIENCE STANDARDS AND EMPLOYEE TRAINING AND RECOGNITION PROGRAMS

If you are a solopreneur, feel free to skip this part.

One of the most effective ways to develop and maintain a customer-centric business is to create customer experience standards. You can write a standards handbook yourself, hire a consultant to create one, or ask an employee committee to develop one collaboratively.

If your small business does not currently have written standards, I believe that involving employees, whether in part or in entirety, can be the most beneficial way to achieve this. Your employees are then empowered to provide their input based on their own experiences with internal and external customers.

If you can afford it, hire a marketing or business consultant to facilitate, work with your team, and keep things on track. The consultant can use employee contributions, as well as her own recommendations, to create a draft and eventually a final standards product that is easy for employees to access and implement. Then on an annual basis, or as the need arises, you can review the standards and make any necessary revisions.

Although the purpose of written standards is to guide employees in their customer interactions on a daily basis, it may be challenging to maintain consistency without adding two more components: employee training and a recognition program. It would be counter-productive for these customer experience standards to sit on a hard drive without regular reference and review. Therefore, it's important to reinforce them consistently and engrain them as part of the company culture.

Initially, a consultant or trainer can conduct a staff workshop to introduce the standards handbook, during which time, she can encourage employees to role-play and discuss 'real-life' customer situations. Many people learn better when there are interactive exercises. Role-playing makes this fun and enables employees to experiment in a safe environment before they use their new skills with customers.

Then, on a semi-annual or annual basis, or as the need arises, plan subsequent workshops that build on and reinforce your standards and tackle new situations. These will also be valuable for any new hires.

To ensure that you have everyone's buy-in, add measurable customer orientation expectations to employee job descriptions and performance reviews. Tie these in with a recognition program and you've closed the loop to ensure customer and brand experience consistency.

TIPS ON ACHIEVING INTERNAL CUSTOMER CENTRISM

If you are a solopreneur, feel free to skip this part.

As with external customers, your small business would not exist without internal customers — its employees. They have tremendous influence on its success or failure. Do you want to take chances, hoping they get it right?

The *2014 Edelman Trust Barometer* demonstrated the importance of internal customer centrism:

How a company treats employees can significantly help – or harm – overall trust. 'Respecting employee rights' is among the top three most important factors positively affecting trust – nearly as critical as ensuring quality control and protecting customer data.

In addition to what I've previously included, here are more tips on how to ensure that your employees stay, feel engaged, and contribute to your small business' success:

- Create a workplace environment that is clean, orderly, healthy, and safe. No one wants to work in a pigsty or feel that his health is at risk by coming to work.

- Ensure that employees know what the business' overarching strategy is and how they can play a role in achieving it.

Bring the company's strategy to life through authentic storytelling, and make every effort to get leaders out of the boardroom and onto the floor, informally connecting with employees. (*2014 Edelman Trust Barometer*)

- Share appropriate resources with employees: blog posts, articles, books, journals, and other educational tools for their areas of responsibility. Encourage them to do the same.

- When the company can prioritize and afford it, offer employees professional development opportunities.

- Make the workplace fun and encourage employee camaraderie.

- Cut employees some slack when necessary. Although separating personal lives from the workplace is important in maintaining professionalism, acknowledge that people are human and we all have bad days as well as challenging life experiences.

- Show compassion and adaptability in cases where people need additional tender loving care (TLC) or consideration. What makes a strong, positive workplace is when team members are supportive of one another.

- Offer shorter work days or the ability to work from home when necessary and feasible. As long as your flexibility and goodwill aren't taken for granted or abused, it's good for business when you treat employees with respect and understand their needs.

Having some freedom would likely help employees accomplish more. Sixty-five percent of workers think a flexible and remote work schedule would increase their productivity. ("New Research Reveals Biggest Productivity Killers for America's Workforce," *The State of Workplace Productivity Report,* Cornerstone OnDemand, 2014)

FOSTERING AUTHENTIC BUSINESS RELATIONSHIPS

Many business and marketing gurus talk about "being authentic," but what does it really mean?

 **Authentic:**
"Not false or copied; genuine; real," (Dictionary.com) which, in the business sense, boils down to individual values and personality.

If you (and employees) are genuine and sincere people, it should be easy to transfer these characteristics to your business lives. When customers discover that you truly care about their needs, you can begin to build relationships of trust. However, if an employee is a distrusting individual by nature, thinking that everyone is out to get him, then this part of the book may take some work.

If your tendency is to greet people warmly, ask questions about their problems or needs, and then make recommendations that will help your customers, then you're on your way. If your suggestions include alternatives to your products and/or services, customers and prospects will appreciate your honesty, improving the chances that they'll come back.

Here's an example:

A former client called to ask me if we could take over an unfinished graphic design project. Her marketing manager had resigned before it was complete, and because her organization had an important upcoming event, she was concerned about the tight deadline.

When she listed the items that required design, I asked some pertinent questions. She initially wanted three designed and printed signs of an event floor plan of attendees' assigned tables. She also wanted admission tickets designed and printed.

"I have a better idea," I advised her. I explained how much nicer it would be to have employees greet guests at each of the three entrances. Each would have a list of attendees, their company names, and their assigned tables. Not only is this a warmer way to guide guests to their seats, it doesn't require graphic design or sign printing... a cost saving.

I also suggested that she forego the tickets. Guests could check in at a registration table where greeters could welcome them and assign their table numbers. She liked that very much.

Yes, it meant that we didn't get that small project, but clients' needs come first. If we can help them save money, time, and effort by NOT using the services they think they need, then we are fostering an authentic relationship of trust. The next time this client requires marketing services, I hope that she'll remember my honest recommendations and come back.

You can have everything in life you want, if you will just help other people get what they want.
(Zig Ziglar)

Another way to foster authentic relationships is to admit when you cannot serve customers. As mentioned previously, if they request certain products or services that your company doesn't offer, you have a choice. You can respond that you can't assist and that's the end of it. OR, you can refer another supplier you know who can. By being helpful, you leave a positive brand impression so the next time they require something, perhaps they'll ask you again.

So where do you find these referrals? When you join your local chamber of commerce and professional or trade associations, you'll gain access to a network of business professionals, some of whom will complement your products and services or compete with them. Working out a mutual referral system for the things your companies cannot provide is good business.

For example:

When I needed a root canal, my dentist referred me to an endodontist for the procedure. Even though he received training in root canals when he was in dental school, he preferred to send his patients to a specialist.

I appreciated going to someone my dentist knew and trusted so I didn't have to start researching for a specialist myself. The procedure went well and I thanked my dentist. His referral added another notch to my trusting relationship with him.

One word of caution on this point, however. There's an inherent risk when referring other suppliers, unless you know that their products or services are top notch. It's your brand reputation on the line. If you're unsure, be honest. Tell people that you can't guarantee the vendor's or professional's quality or service and that they should do their own due diligence.

The referral system is especially effective if you join any small business leads or referral groups. These networks focus on sharing good quality business leads among members. The philosophy behind the concept is that the more leads and referrals you make, the more your business will benefit from others' leads and referrals.

As beneficial as these networks can be, they can also present some hurdles. When I first relocated to Phoenix, I networked like crazy, trying to meet new people and seek out opportunities. When I launched my own business, I attended a couple of leads groups to test them.

I tried my best to offer quality leads to other members, but since I was relatively new in town, I was at a disadvantage. Besides feeling an underlying pressure to produce leads, I was hesitant about referring others to group members.

I had absolutely no firsthand knowledge of their products or services. How could I possibly know how good they were? Since my reputation was also at stake, I decided to rely on organic word of mouth and marketing instead and share what I could with those who asked.

That doesn't mean your personal experience with a leads group will be negative. Some have proven to be very successful. Try one out and assess if it works for your company.

Offering advice, sharing your expertise and passion, and being a *mensch* are ways you can help others get what they want. I'm not suggesting that you give it all away for free, but giving some of it away, without expectation, can make you a star in others' eyes. That's how you build thought leadership and attract customers.

 **Mensch**
Yiddish for human being or someone of integrity.

Being yourself and not feeling the need to put on airs can help build authentic business relationships. You know your business products and/or services won't be the ideal fit for everyone, so why change your style and approach to suit the ones that don't?

The people you want to work with will appreciate your unique style, brand, and honesty. Consistency is what they learn to bank on — not the latest fad. Be genuine and you'll find greater opportunities when people discover you and then stick around.

Being authentic also includes communicating regularly with customers to demonstrate your concern and interest in their personal and business lives. Use social media, e-mail, handwritten postcards or notes, and other communication tools to reach out to them.

IDEA #2 TAKEAWAY

Always be customer focused. No exceptions. Your business exists for its customers. You make a living from its customers. You have a roof over your head because of its customers.

Say this phrase to yourself whenever you feel frustrated: "My customers *are* my business."

So when you (and your employees) unconditionally believe that your customers are the reason you get up in the morning and why the business exists, you are well on your way to small business branding success.

customer-focused

IDEA #3

GET MARKETING AND BRANDING HELP WHEN YOU NEED IT

Maybe you know a lot about marketing, branding, and running a business, or maybe you don't. The way things work today, it's almost impossible to be an expert at everything, even within the same disciplines. Just within the marketing and branding world, there are numerous specialty areas, such as:

- Business branding
- Business-to-business marketing
- Business-to-consumer marketing
- Cause marketing
- Channel marketing
- Content marketing
- Digital marketing
- Direct marketing
- Direct mail marketing
- E-mail marketing
- Employer branding
- Event marketing
- Guerilla marketing

- Inbound marketing
- In-store marketing
- Integrated marketing
- Interactive marketing
- Internal marketing
- Internet marketing
- Loyalty marketing
- Marketing communications
- Mobile marketing
- Multichannel marketing
- One-to-one marketing
- Outbound marketing
- Personal branding
- Product branding
- Product marketing
- Promotional marketing
- Relationship marketing
- Rebranding
- Sales and marketing
- Search engine marketing
- Services branding
- Services marketing
- Social media marketing
- Strategic marketing
- Word-of-mouth marketing

The list can go on and it can change quickly, too. Many of these specialty areas didn't exist a few years ago. Even though your business may start out without a marketing or branding budget, it may eventually grow to require both internal and external specialists to help it succeed.

In my experience, small business owners appear more willing to hire certain types of specialists with less hesitation than others. Legal counsel is a good example. Although there are online resources to set up a business, register a trademark, and form a partnership, many small business owners realize that they will occasionally need access to an attorney, and so they budget for legal fees.

Even if small business owners do their own bookkeeping, they will often hire an accountant to prepare their taxes. They'll definitely hire a computer specialist when their screens go black or a virus has eaten their data! But for some reason, marketing and branding are specialties that many small business people try doing themselves – or avoid altogether.

It's true that when little revenue is coming in, it isn't feasible to hire the caliber of marketing professionals you may need. On the other hand, when your small business is generating enough revenue, it's wise to create an annual marketing plan and allocate expenses to hire or outsource professionals.

It's especially important for companies seeking business loans, angel investors, or venture capitalists to have a written business and marketing and branding plan. Without preparing a comprehensive plan, it can be more challenging to access investment money.

So where does this leave the millions of small businesses that have marketing and branding needs but not enough money to hire an agency or a consultant?

LEARN WHAT YOU CAN

Learn as much as you can about marketing and branding on your own. Even after the business can afford internal or outsourced specialists, some basic knowledge is highly valuable for small business owners and managers.

CLASSES, SEMINARS, AND WEBINARS

A good start is to take classes and/or seminars. Many local community colleges and universities offer a variety of small business marketing and branding courses. Some require in-person participation, while others are available online.

GOVERNMENT AGENCIES AND NONPROFIT ORGANIZATIONS

Check for government agencies and nonprofit organizations that assist small businesses with dedicated microsites, business development centers, classes, or one-to-one consultations or coaching. Start with your city, state, province, or federal government website.

Here are some US resources:

- National Federation of Independent Business
- SCORE
- US Small Business Administration

In Canada:

- Canada Business Network
- Canadian Federation of Independent Business
- Service Canada

MARKETING VENDORS

Look for free white papers, e-books, and webinars from reputable marketing and branding vendors that offer free resources for their own lead generation purposes. There's no obligation on your part to use their services, but if you find their content valuable, share them on social media and with colleagues to help them gain exposure and search engine ranking. That's a sure way of showing your appreciation for their expertise.

BOOKS, BLOGS, AND WEBSITES

Regularly read marketing, branding, and customer-focused books, blogs, and websites to gain insight, learn new ideas, discover new tools, and dialog with experts. Here are just a few of the many good blogs to read:

- *Attention Getting Marketing*
- *Branding & Marketing*
- *Branding Strategy Insider*
- *Business 2 Community*
- *Damn, I Wish I'd Thought of That!*
- *Drew's Marketing Minute*
- *Duct Tape Marketing*
- *Jeffbullas's Blog*
- *MarketingProfs*
- *Seth's Blog*
- *Shep Hyken's Customer Service Blog*
- *SmallBizClub*

- *SmallBizDaily*
- *SmallBizTrends*
- *Small Business Marketing from OPEN Forum*®
- *Social Media Examiner*
- *Social Media Today*
- *WebInkNow*
- *WebMarketingToday*

SOCIAL MEDIA, ASSOCIATIONS, AND CHAMBERS OF COMMERCE

Join selected marketing and branding LinkedIn groups, question sites, small business associations, and/or chambers of commerce. They offer countless ways to learn more about marketing and branding.

In active LinkedIn groups, group members post resources and share their expertise, advice, and opinions in discussion forums. You can ask questions and share your own best practices.

On sites like AllExperts, Answerbag, askville (by Amazon), Quora, and Yahoo! Answers, you can post your marketing and branding questions and have peers and experts respond. If you discover members with consistently good answers, you can choose to follow them, sign up for their e-mails, and access any free or low-cost webinars or publications they offer.

There are several small business associations across the country, some with national and local presences. Many offer marketing and branding resources, conferences, training, and educational programs.

Chambers of commerce are also excellent groups to access marketing/branding professional development opportunities and resources. They also offer valuable networking opportunities and can add credibility and exposure to your business, increasing its referrals.

A 2012 study by The Schapiro Group and Market Street Services showed:

When consumers know that a small business is a member of their local chamber of commerce, they are 44% more likely to think favorably of it, and they're a full 63% more likely to purchase goods or services from that company in the future.

Join or start a mastermind group or alliance. According to The Success Alliance, mastermind groups:

Offer a combination of masterminding, peer brainstorming, education, accountability and support in a group setting to sharpen your business and personal skills. A mastermind group helps you and your mastermind group members achieve success.

Being part of a mastermind group of small business owners or professionals can give you the opportunity to learn marketing best practices, tools, and ideas that others have used successfully. You can meet in person locally, or join out-of-town members using electronic platforms such as Skype or other video-conferencing programs.

Suppose you and/or your employees just don't have the time or inclination to learn about marketing and branding or join a group? Perhaps you're too busy managing business operations, sales, and customer service.

DO SOME RESEARCH

BARTERING

Ask your network if anyone knows of a marketing or branding agency that is willing to barter its expertise for your company's goods or services. You can also explore online bartering exchanges such as Barter Business Unlimited, BizX, Itex, and SwapRight.com or check similar local groups. There's even an association – International Reciprocal Trade Association – dedicated to ethical standards in trading and bartering.

HIGHER EDUCATION

When you want to conduct marketing research or develop a marketing and branding strategy, check out local universities with entrepreneur and/or marketing programs. Some have professor-supervised, student consulting groups that will work on your project for free or a smaller fee than hiring professional consultants or agencies.

For smaller projects, look into college marketing and communications departments for students who would welcome a paid opportunity to add to their portfolios and practical work experience. Ask their professors or instructors for references to ensure students are good matches for your projects. To ensure that students' work is worthy of implementation, perhaps their instructors would be amenable to reviewing student results for an affordable fee.

There's also a website devoted to getting your problems "solved by the brightest college students in the world." NoodleStorm is free and confidential to use and includes universities such as Harvard University, Stanford University, Columbia University, Texas A&M University, and UCLA.

INTERNSHIPS

Hiring student interns during the summer or after graduation is another way to gain low-cost marketing and branding assistance. Some universities offer subsidies to employers for hiring their students. You can also investigate state and provincial grant programs.

If your small business is in Canada, the federal government funds supervised, career-related work experience for young workers to develop their skills and knowledge. Businesses can get up to 50% subsidy of an intern's summer minimum wages. Contact Mentor Works.

In the US, read the Department of Labor's Fact Sheet on "Internship Programs Under The Fair Labor Standards Act" to learn about paid versus unpaid internships. There may be legal ramifications to hiring unpaid interns.

Another option is to look for new immigrant employment programs. Because many immigrants find it challenging to obtain employment in their fields without local work experience, they often look for internships to gain a foothold in the labor market.

There may be solid candidates in your area who have marketing and branding experience from their countries of origin. At the end of these placements, employers can hire their interns or write referral letters and say goodbye.

For example:

I hired a new immigrant worker when I headed the marketing department of a large nonprofit organization. (Similar to small businesses, most nonprofits must be creative when accessing necessary resources.) I applied to a program that funded the intern's salary for a three- to six-month period, as long as I provided mentor support and professional development opportunities.

I was lucky. The woman who joined my marketing team was amazing. Her editing and proofreading skills went beyond what we native English speakers could muster! She was such a good marketing communications specialist that I adjusted my budget to hire her permanently. We are still friends, 14 years later.

FREELANCERS

You can also explore freelance websites that allow you to post a specific marketing project and the maximum budget you are willing to pay. Then sit back and wait for freelancer proposals to arrive.

This is a good way to access marketing professionals who may have time for extra projects, are starting out and need to gain hands-on experience, or want new clients, especially when business is slow. Some sites include Fiverr, Guru, UpWork, and Workhoppers.

One request: Please don't use sites where freelancers do the work first in order to "win" your job. Think about it. It's very unfair and takes advantage of people, many of whom live in third-world countries. Check their portfolios and references first and then award your project.

When you have a burning marketing or branding question, want to discuss an idea you have, or need advice, there are sites where you can pay fees by the minute to access a variety of experts on an as-needed basis. One such site is Clarity and another is Ether.

HIRING A MARKETING AND BRANDING CONSULTANT OR AGENCY

When your business can afford to pay for external help, a marketing and branding consultant or agency can give your small business the resources it requires. Professionals can help develop your marketing and branding plan, produce print and electronic marketing communications collateral, write content for your blog or website, and take care of countless other marketing tactics.

You can also hire marketing and branding consultants on retainer to advise your small business, extend your existing marketing department, or effectively become your marketing team when you can't afford to hire permanent staff.

ADVANTAGES

- Marketing consultants can develop and implement your marketing and branding strategy and tactics.

- They can guide and advise you, recommending effective options for your business needs, within your budget limitations.

- They can give your business an objective opinion, perspective, and open-mindedness, free of internal dynamics.

- They can provide your business with insights gained from many years of hands-on experience.

- They enable your business to delegate marketing responsibilities so it can focus on operations and sales.

- You only pay for the time or project in which the consultant or agency performs tasks on your behalf. You don't have to cover benefits, vacation time, or coffee breaks and you can put them on hold when business declines or your project is complete.

CAUTIONS

- Don't hire a less experienced or "cheap" marketing consultant or agency that can't produce the quality results you expect or require. You don't want to use lackluster or unprofessional work because redoing things later with someone else will be costly. Doing it right the first time can maximize your return on investment (ROI).

- Don't hire a consultant or agency without checking references. You may discover that as talented as they may be, they could have poor business conduct that will hinder the relationship.

- Don't hire the first consultant or agency that someone recommends. It's a good idea to explore three to five of them to ensure a good fit. Ask each the same questions in interviews as you would when hiring employees. When working with an agency, find out who will be your direct liaison or account manager and who will be working on your project. It's much easier to communicate with one individual.

- Don't try to juggle different niche marketing specialists on your own unless you have a sound background in marketing. You know what they say about too many cooks in the kitchen.

› Work with a good marketing generalist or agency that can oversee and project manage specialists on your behalf. Your business needs a cohesive, integrated, and holistic approach to marketing and branding.

- Don't expect to find consultants who will work for free. Professionals have to support their families and cover overhead costs like other business owners. Unlike salaried employees, they're responsible for their own insurance, office expenses, and administrative duties. Ask consultants and agencies if they offer a small business discount unless, of course, all their clients are small businesses.

- Don't meet with consultants under the guise of interviewing them for contracted work. Picking their brains when you have no budget or intent to hire them is not only unethical, it's very unfair.

- Don't work with consultants who conduct themselves unprofessionally. Similar to hiring employees, certain characteristics and behaviors speak of their credibility and brand.

> One such area to evaluate involves their initial proposals. If they send their quotes in casual e-mails, without an attached bio, supporting materials, or official quotations, it might be a hint that they aren't concerned about presenting professionally.

> This is a red flag that could apply to other areas of work they do for your business. After all, you want to work with professionals who excel at marketing and branding. If they don't present their own brand well, don't even bother.

- Don't work with consultants or agencies without a written agreement that spells out expectations, deliverables, fees, and terms and conditions for the consulting contract. They should present you with this agreement once you make a verbal commitment to move forward.

  > If you're interviewing several consultants or agencies, ask how they intend to solidify the working relationship. This way, you can see which ones use written agreements as standard protocol.

- Don't delegate marketing and branding responsibilities to others and then disappear. Regular, open communication is crucial in achieving your company's objectives. Be honest, share your feedback, and quickly address any issues or barriers that need attention.

- If the relationship doesn't work out, there should be an 'out' clause in the agreement. It's best to cut ties earlier than later if things aren't gelling.

- Don't micromanage consultants. It is as counter-productive as delegating responsibilities and disappearing.

- Don't hire a marketing and branding consultant and then 'park' the work she completed. This is not in your company's best interests. If implementing a plan or project isn't part of your agreement, negotiate with her to do the rest or hire someone who can.

- Don't treat consultants or agencies poorly. They can be your greatest assets and brand ambassadors when you cultivate a partnership with them.

  › The longer you work with the same consultants, the easier it is to develop a positive, working friendship. Some will give you extra time and effort without charging you, based on a trusting, long-term relationship.

  › If you're unsure whether you are demanding too much, ask about their boundaries upfront and try to stay within them. Expecting weekend, evening, holiday, or rush work is a good example. You want to be able to count on them when you need them, so respecting their time and personal lives will go far.

- Don't expect consultants or agencies to produce everything you need when you can't afford it all. Be realistic and do your marketing and branding processes in stages, prioritizing as you go.

IDEA #3 TAKEAWAY

Remember, the more you can budget and invest in marketing and branding expertise to reach and engage your target audiences with the right frequency, relevance, consistency, and professionalism, the sooner your business can build and sustain a strong brand for success.

INVEST in marketing.

IDEA #4

PROFESSIONALISM PAYS OFF

When you are the customer, in which businesses do you have more faith and confidence? A company whose employees appear to be presentable, knowledgeable, caring, and attentive to you, or one that has slovenly looking staff who don't seem to know the answers to your questions nor seem to care? Of course, you'd choose the former.

Professionalism is not just an idea; it's a big deal. Having a team of dedicated and professional staff makes a huge difference in how customers perceive your business, repeatedly patronize it, and refer it to others. It can make or break your business brand whether you are a sole proprietor, have one employee, or employ a hundred people.

Here are a few ways to safeguard your small business' level of professionalism:

MAINTAIN A CLEAN, TIDY, AND SAFE WORK ENVIRONMENT

Maintaining a professional workplace contributes to your company's brand reputation and service delivery quality. Customers and employees may not say anything, but if your place of business is a mess or unsafe, it can leave a negative impression. Desktops should not look like a war zone and garbage receptacles should be emptied regularly.

This also includes the company's restrooms. Imagine a prospect or customer asking to use the bathroom and discovering filth or disarray. It's enough to gross them out and send them away with a negative brand impression that you can never win back. Yuck!

Many years ago, I was shopping in a national department store that had just been renovated. I browsed every department at my leisure, poking around the glitzy, new fixtures and displays with relaxed enjoyment – until I had to use the restroom.

The bathrooms hadn't been touched! The company had invested in its floor space but had totally neglected the one area where cleanliness and modernity really counted. The 1950s-style cracked toilets and broken tiling left such a bad impression with me that I am recounting this story almost 30 years later! We don't forget.

Employees can have the same negative experiences in the workplace. Aside from being grossed out, clutter, dirt, and foul odors can be psychologically damaging to them, possibly reducing productivity and motivation. The mess can affect employees' physical health, increasing absenteeism and healthcare costs. Workers with allergies or asthma won't stay long if a workplace makes them sick. Your location has much to gain from a pleasant and clean environment.

According to *Healthy Beginnings Magazine*:

Cluttered and untidy workspaces can reduce productivity. It can be very distracting to work around needless clutter. If there is a lot of dust lurking in corners and on shelves, it is a sign of old stagnant energy that needs to be cleared out. Dirty work spaces communicate a lack of attention to detail to the customer, and sometimes much worse.

Additionally, a tidy workplace is a safer one. It's easy to trip or become injured when things are out of place or are stored insecurely. According to the US Department of Labor, Occupational Safety & Health Administration:

Injuries and illnesses increase workers' compensation and retraining costs, absenteeism, and faulty product. They also decrease productivity, morale, and profits.

Safe workplaces provide the consistency and reliability needed to build a community and grow a business. Workplaces with active safety and health leadership have fewer injuries, are often rated 'better places to work,' and have more satisfied, more productive employees. These employees return to work more quickly after an injury or illness and produce higher-quality products and services.

Besides, workplaces that establish safety and health management systems can reduce their injury and illness costs by 20%–40%! Now that's a good incentive.

Another factor to consider comes from the *2014 Edelman Trust Barometer* and affects external trust for your company:

Having sub-standard work conditions is among the most damaging factors (to trust), along with displaying unethical business practices, exposing customer data and acting irresponsibly during a crisis.

When your place of business looks clean and tidy and is a safe place to work, it sends a message of professionalism and presents positive brand experiences to both internal and external customers.

APPEARANCES COUNT

First impressions count and your attire, grooming, and overall appearance are definitely part of those initial brand impressions when serving customers in person. Appearances can also affect perceptions and behavior.

In a 2010 *Psychology Today* article, Audrey Nelson, Ph.D., mentioned that our attire conveys messages of how we want to be seen.

Fifty years of research that tells us you can change perceptions of a person by changing their clothes. There is no getting around it. Dress has persuasive value that influences the behavior of others. Clothing may influence the extent to which another person may consider us credible. It is often read as a sign of character.

Other interesting findings about work clothing:

- When wearing perceived high-status clothing, people gained cooperation from others more easily and scored job recommendations and higher salaries.

- Participants watching one man video interviewing for a job on two separate occasions, rated one better than the other. When the man wore a shirt with a designer logo, they found him more suitable for the job and deserving of a 9% higher salary than when he wore a shirt without a logo. Is it fair? No, but it's reality.

- Dressing more casually can reduce stress and increase collaborative activity. (Eva Rykrsmith, "Dress Code or Not, What You Wear Matters," *The Fast Track*, May 23, 2012)

- Women in high-level positions who dress in what is seen as sexy attire are viewed as less competent, regardless of their skill sets. These women are passed over for promotions more often than their more modestly dressed female colleagues. (Laura Sinberg, "What Not To Wear To Work," *Forbes*, July, 22, 2009)

So should your business define a dress code policy to ensure brand consistency? There are two schools of thought on this.

If you are a solopreneur, feel free to skip this part.

Some companies consider dress codes passé, believing that if they hire mature, intelligent employees, they will know what's acceptable to wear and what is not. Recent discrimination lawsuits have added to this issue, causing further reticence by some employers to impose dress codes at all.

Others still prefer dress code standards, with some degree of flexibility. So whether you expect your employees to don suits, business casual, or jeans, it doesn't hurt to clarify what is acceptable in writing.

The nature and location of your business are both factors in determining its wardrobe expectations. Companies located in warm climates are typically more *laissez-faire* in terms of dress standards. It wouldn't be unusual to see a New York City professional wearing a suit in the summer when the temperature is 97°F/36°C plus humidity. But it will be atypical for those living in Florida or Arizona.

Regional norms can also affect employee attire expectations. What is characteristic on the North American west coast may not work on the east coast.

If uniforms are typical for your industry, your dress code standards are much easier to manage. Adding screen-printed or embroidered logos on company uniforms can boost brand awareness.

Unless your customers are in luxury or high-end corporate markets or in formal work environments, you can't expect employees to be fashionistas. However, you can expect them to be neat and tidy in their physical appearances.

Here's a list of questions to consider when proposing dress codes to improve professionalism:

- Footwear: Would you allow sneakers, sandals, or flip-flops on the job?

- Tops: Is it acceptable to permit employees to wear T-shirts, halter tops, camisoles, tank tops, shirts worn over pants, sheer blouses/dresses, or sundresses?

- Headwear: Is wearing baseball caps or head scarves (for nonreligious reasons) OK?

- Bottoms: Would you discourage shorts, crop pants, jeans, khakis, and short skirts?

- Branded clothing: Would you find it acceptable when employees wear attire with corporate or product logos and/or messaging – from brands other than yours?

- How do you define what's over the top (no pun intended): heavy makeup; loud jewelry; visible tattoos; nose, eye, lip, or tongue piercings; exposed cleavage or torso skin; ill-fitting clothing (e.g. popping buttons, overly tight); or exposed undergarments?

- How accepting will your business be for clothing differences related to sexual orientation, culture, gender, race, or ethnicity? You will need to check for employment standards legislation in your location before making these decisions.

It's important to enlist employees' input in this process to give them a sense of ownership and increase compliance. You may also want to ask a few of your good customers what they would find offensive. Just remember not to kowtow to prejudice.

COMPANY VEHICLES

If your company operates delivery or service vehicles or you drive a car with company advertising, the lettering and vehicle wraps reflect your brand's appearance, too. It's always best to use professionally designed graphics.

Driving behaviors can also affect brand impressions. When you (or employees) drive company vehicles irresponsibly, giving other drivers "the finger," speeding, running red lights, or cutting people off, you are definitely sending unprofessional messages, to say the least. Plus, consider the liability issue when employees aren't practicing safe driving habits.

There's a good chance that you or managers may not learn about these incidents unless you place a "How's my driving?" decal on company vehicles. A Transportation Research Board study (2011) found that vehicles displaying the decal were involved in 22% fewer accidents and resulted in a 52% reduction in accident-related costs. It's definitely worth your while as long as someone is ready and willing to receive call complaints or you have an appropriate messaging system.

SIGNAGE

Outdoor and indoor signage is as important as your company's other marketing collateral. In fact, your company's signage may be the first representation of its brand that customers and prospects see. Ensure signs are consistent with brand identity standards and professionally designed.

BUSINESS ETIQUETTE

Etiquette and manners are lessons we learn from our parents as children, no matter what our socioeconomic backgrounds are. Sadly, too many people missed out on good instructions, leaving them at a disadvantage in the workplace.

Even though you may hire polite people with sound business knowledge, it may be prudent to include business etiquette best practices in your employee handbook to outline the company's expectations. Here are some examples:

- This may be obvious, but saying 'please' and 'thank you' are always in order.

- Keep noise to a minimum in an office setting. Loud voices and conversations can be distracting for those trying to concentrate.

- Don't take credit for something you did not do. When you work on collaborative projects, always mention the others involved.

- Limit personal calls. In close quarters, they can be annoying to your colleagues.

- Be punctual for meetings and appointments. When you're running late or need to cancel, call to inform the meeting planner at the earliest possible time.

- Respect everyone, regardless of their titles or positions. Not only is it the right thing to do, you also never know with whom your path will cross down the road.

- Avoid using juvenile or offensive cell phone ringtones in business settings.

- Avoid interrupting colleagues when they're on the phone or in meetings, unless there's a valid reason.

- Don't work on your computer while on a business call or in a meeting with someone. This conveys very rude behavior.

- When you meet people for the first time, shake their hands, smile, and make eye contact. They're judging your personal and company brand at that moment.

Many more online resources are available on this subject, as well as specialists who offer business etiquette and protocol training. If your company has customers in other countries, cross-cultural consultants can advise you on appropriate etiquette, customs, and protocol, or check out a free online guide called "Culture Crossing Guide."

CUSTOMER COMMUNICATION

Responding to customers quickly, whether by telephone, e-mail, social media, website, chat, or other channels is imperative to your company's level of professionalism and its brand reputation. It's important to reply in the channels people have used to contact you, so having protocols for each channel you offer is a wise move.

It's also smart to gauge which channels your customers prefer, even if you don't use them yet. Once a channel reaches a tipping point, your company needs to stay in the game and adopt the ones that customers favor.

TELEPHONE

If we accept a 2Talk.com, November 2014 study, "Consumer Behaviors Towards Multi-Channel Customer Service," then the telephone still reigns as the most widely used channel for customer service. Yes, this old-fashioned, Alexander Graham Bell invention is preferred by 33.5% of consumers to resolve customer service issues.

No matter how you personally feel on any given day, your telephone communication must be consistent and represent your company's brand. Here are some professional phone tips:

- Answer the phone within three rings.

- Swallow any food or drink before you pick up the telephone.

- Greet callers with a smile and identify yourself with your name, department and/or company name, followed by "How can I help you?" (You'll be surprised how others will pick up on your smile just from the tone of your voice.) Company greetings should be standardized for brand consistency.

- Similarly, develop a standardized closing that is positive and friendly, no matter how callers behaved during the conversation.

- Speak clearly so callers can fully understand you. This is especially important if you talk too quickly or have a regional or foreign accent. Customers may get annoyed when they have to ask you to repeat yourself several times. If that happens, pretend you're an actor on stage and enunciate your words, speaking slower.

- Be warm, inviting, enthusiastic, and friendly.

- Speaking in a monotone voice sends a negative message that you're bored. Put some personality into it!

- Always allow callers to finish their thoughts before jumping in.

- If you need to use your hands in order to serve callers, ask first before using the speakerphone.

- When taking messages for colleagues, you don't need to share why they are unavailable. It's more professional to simply mention their unavailability at the moment.

  › When colleagues are off work due to illness or are out of town, use your discretion whether to reveal that information for privacy and security reasons.

- Take notes when appropriate so you can follow up easily or pass the information to a colleague.

- Ask customers if it's OK when you need to put them on hold. Check back with them every 30–40 seconds if your task takes longer than that.

- When transferring callers, explain why and to whom. "I'm going to transfer you to Juanita. She handles all our [fill in] and can help you with that."

- When people call for information that is easily available on your website, avoid saying, "That information is available on our website."

  › Of course, these calls are interruptions for you, but that's irrelevant. You have no idea why these callers didn't check online first. Maybe they have disabilities, their computers are malfunctioning or broken, or they can't afford their own computers.

    » Don't make assumptions and embarrass them. Use these opportunities to win them over with your pleasant customer service. Innocuous questions may lead to new business!

- Always ensure that you (or someone else) fulfill what you promise to callers.

- Your telephone answering and messaging system should set the tone for doing business with your company. An unanswered phone is unprofessional and may imply that your business is unreliable if prospects and customers cannot reach you during business hours or they're calling from a different time zone.

- Record a voicemail message that includes your name and a call to action, such as asking callers to leave a message with specific information.

- Check your voicemail at regular intervals.

- Return all voicemail messages within 24 hours (or sooner if you can).

- Change your voicemail message if you'll be away from the office, indicating whom to contact in your absence. If you don't do this, callers won't hear back from you until you return from vacation or illness. Not only is it unprofessional, by that time, it can be too late.

- If you're a sole proprietor or an employee with a mobile phone as your sole business line, make sure that you answer when there are no distracting noises such as crying babies, grocery carts colliding, cash registers ringing, etc. These sounds can give customers an unprofessional impression of the business.

  > Besides, it isn't very appealing or professional when you talk to clients within earshot of the people around you. One of my pet peeves is hearing someone's business cell phone conversation while walking the aisles of a retail store. Frankly, I find it rude and it infringes on my personal space.

ONLINE CHAT

Online chat has certainly matured as a customer communication channel over the past few years. It can cut your business' customer support costs; improve response times; increase leads, sales, and brand loyalty; and provide valuable customer feedback and information. If you have an e-commerce site, online chat can also lead to increased customer purchases.

Taking advantage of this technology effectively will depend on the nature of your small business. As there are many available chat options and features, I recommend you do your due diligence before deciding on the best fit for your business.

One cautionary note... ensure you have ample coverage to manage online chat tools. It would certainly be unprofessional to offer a chat window that's offline most of the time.

As for customer communication norms, chat service is similar to other channels when it comes to polite, patient, and friendly service. But because it takes place in real time, and is a written conversation, chatters must have excellent writing skills and be able to manage several customer chats simultaneously.

Here are some tips to ensure professionalism in your customers' chat experiences:

- Ensure you train chat operators with the knowledge they'll need to serve customers and answer their questions effectively. Having sales skills is also of great benefit.

- Ensure you can customize the chat window to accommodate your business' brand colors and identity.

- Add the chat feature to web pages in a position where visitors can easily discover it. However, do not customize it to jump out at visitors annoyingly.

- When you first address chat visitors and during conversations, use their names to personalize the experience.

- Be human and warm, allowing your personality to shine.

- Use short conversational sentences with proper grammar and spelling, avoiding jargon, acronyms, and slang.

- It's OK to use "canned" responses (pre-scripted messages) whenever they apply. Just make sure that they sound human and not robotic.

- When operators do not know the answers to specific questions, they can either ask customers to wait while they check with someone else or offer to have a coworker contact them directly by e-mail or telephone, whichever customers prefer.

- Don't close the chat window until customers indicate that their issues or questions have been resolved.

Several inexpensive chat programs are available for small businesses, including ClickDesk, ContactUs, and My Live Chat.

E-MAIL

E-mail is still a ubiquitous form of communication in the workplace. Since this channel has been with us a lot longer than other electronic communications, many believe that they have a solid grasp of it. Just in case you need a refresher, here are some e-mail communication tips that can increase your company's level of professionalism:

- When you compose e-mails or responses, use the same professional tone and wording as if you were writing a letter. Once you develop more established relationships, you can eventually take a more informal approach.

- As with other channels, use full sentences and correct grammar, punctuation, and spelling. Avoid jargon and acronyms that recipients may not recognize.

- Avoid lengthy explanations and long-winded messages. If a matter is more detailed or more effectively resolved in person or by telephone, offer to take the conversation offline.

- Today, people read e-mails using a variety of devices. Avoid unusual fonts, opting for the most common ones instead. I actually recommend using sans-serif fonts such as Arial, Calibri, Tahoma, and Trebuchet, which are easier to read in the digital space.

- Remember that your e-mails can be forwarded, so ensure that anything you say is accurate and respectful or they can come back to bite you. There may also be legal implications to what you put in writing.

- Do not include private information in e-mails. It is not a secure communication channel. Respecting your customers' privacy also has legal consequences and certainly demonstrates your level of professionalism when handled properly.

- Always review your e-mails before you hit "send." It's amazing how many little boo-boos you can find that can affect customers' brand perceptions. Use a spelling and grammar checker in your e-mail software program.

- Unless you are away from the office, avoid using the e-mail autoresponder. Another one of my pet peeves is receiving a return message that says something like this:

  "I am very busy now and cannot reply to your e-mail for the next two weeks." You may as well close up shop. We're all busy.

  When you're on vacation or sick, use the autoresponder to leave someone else's contact information for customer assistance in your absence.

- If you have a contact form on your business website, set it to forward automatically to a specific, monitored e-mail address. I can remember completing some of these forms in past years and never receiving a reply. Did they want my business or not?

- When people haven't articulated their entire inquiry or problem, ask for clarification with specific questions.

- If you cannot respond immediately, acknowledge receiving the e-mail and indicate when you will reply.

- Use the blind copy option (Bcc) sparingly. Not everyone who is blind copied will catch it. You don't want them replying when they shouldn't.

- Ensure that all employees use the same e-mail signature template for brand consistency.

- Remember that e-mail communication can easily be misconstrued because there are no voice inflections or body language to accompany them. Be careful when using benign sarcasm or humor.

SOCIAL MEDIA

More companies are using social media (SM) channels than ever before. According to Michael Stelzner in the *2015 Social Media Marketing Industry Report: How Marketers Are Using Social Media to Grow Their Businesses*, a significant 92% of marketers said that social media was important to their businesses.

Yet companies delivering customer care and support through social media networks achieved far superior annual gains (7.5%), compared to their peers (2.9%). Moreover, they enjoyed a 5.4% annual increase in the number of positive mentions of their products or services through SM channels. (*Social Customer Care: Steps to Success in 2014*, Aberdeen Group)

B2B companies have lagged behind B2C in SM adoption but are catching up due to the more recent emphasis on content marketing. Since relationship building is key to small business success, SM gives your business another channel in which to reach out and communicate with its audiences.

Professionalism is as important here as in any other channel. Here are some social media tips to maintain professionalism in your communication:

- If you have more than one person representing your brand on SM, develop protocols to guide them. All it takes is one slip up and a company's brand reputation is toast.

- Segregate your personal SM accounts from those you use for business purposes. Your customers will be uninterested in your newest recipe unless your business is food related. They certainly won't feel confident in a company that posts its owner's drinking binge photo. Use common sense.

- When customers send you direct messages, be sure to respond within the same day whenever possible. Check your SM accounts regularly or at scheduled times.

- Share worthwhile content related to your business.

- Don't get too chummy or overly familiar with customers on SM. Remember that outside of direct messages, others can read your posts and comments.

- Avoid jokes, religious or political content, or anything that your audiences may deem controversial or offensive. You don't want to alienate people.

- Always respond to negative and positive customer feedback in a timely fashion. For complaints, you may want to apologize and ask to take the issue offline, especially on Twitter. It's challenging to go back and forth using 140 characters. Use the techniques I covered in Idea #2.

ETHICS AND BEHAVIOR

Even though small business is one of the most trusted US institutions (according to 2015 Gallup poll on confidence in US institutions), a small company that behaves unethically or unprofessionally will ultimately lose customers and employees.

Professionalism in your workplace relies on establishing parameters on what is suitable office behavior and decorum and what isn't. Of course, you'll want to create an enjoyable and lively work environment, but sometimes limits are necessary to avoid team acrimony and misunderstandings.

Deciding on what's acceptable will depend on your industry or profession. For example, a boutique design studio or technology company can have very laid-back cultures. It wouldn't be unusual to hear swearing, music, and employees playing games on breaks. On the other hand, if your business is more formal, then expectations will be quite different.

Some standards questions you may want to consider include:

- Is snacking or lunching at open-concept desks acceptable?

- How do you intend to discourage office gossip?

- Are employees encouraged to report misconduct to management or the business owner?

- How do you handle it when employees abuse their breaks or lunch times?

- Is smoking allowed in break rooms, near entrances, etc.?

- Do you have clearly identified privacy, confidentiality, and records management policies?

- Does your business have standards that reinforce sexual harassment and discrimination laws?

- How will your business handle conflicts of interest?

- Does your business have policies against bribes, favors, or other unethical employee behaviors?

- Does your business have tipping, gift, moonlighting, business credit card use, customer database sharing, business property borrowing, and SM usage policies?

You can find many sample codes of ethics online, so I'll add just a few guidelines here.

- Don't discuss your employees, customers, or prospects in public. No matter where you live and work, it's not worth the chance that someone will overhear you and know exactly who you're discussing. Now that's unprofessional.

- Avoid being lured into unethical or uncomfortable situations by well-paying prospects or customers. No amount of money can ever erase the unprofessionalism of doing or saying something you'll regret later.

- Avoid discussing controversial subjects with business colleagues, customers, and prospects unless you know them very well and are on friendly terms. Your business can quickly get cut off if you're on the "wrong" side of a religious, political, or social issue.

- Punctuality and respect for others' time is a crucial component of professionalism. Communicate when you're going to be late. Show up early for meetings.

- "Ethical drift" can easily erode your brand.

Ethical Drift:

"The gradual ebbing of standards that can occur in an individual, a group, or an organization as a result of environmental pressures. It often occurs insidiously, and even without conscious awareness. Just as a boat adrift in the midst of the ocean can travel long distances without any visible change in its location, so too can ethical drift occur without people realizing that they have changed (usually for the worse) their ethical standards." (Psychologist, Dr. J. Sternberg 2012)

Bottom line – avoid doing unethical things "just this once," as they can easily become habit forming and lead you down a slippery slope to brand erosion and possible business failure. Aside from taking risks with your brand reputation, some unethical conduct also happens to be illegal.

Some unethical examples that can affect your business negatively:

- false advertising
- not honoring warranties or guarantees
- substituting substandard goods or parts
- short-changing on services
- copying or plagiarizing from competitors
- "fudging" accounting records
- overbilling for products or services
- falsifying business records

According to Michael Josephson (2013), founder and president of Josephson Institute Center for Business Ethics:

Managers prove themselves to be leaders when they do what is right, even when it costs more than they want to pay, because they understand that the cost of losing credibility and moral authority outweighs the benefits of expedient compromise.

BUSINESS DOCUMENTS AND WRITTEN COMMUNICATION

If providing quotations, estimates, or proposals is part of your small business' operations, it is more professional to prepare them in written format using a company template. The same applies to invoices and most business documents. These materials should adhere to your company's brand identity standards guidelines, consistent with its other collateral.

Although it's tempting to use easily available design templates, most are too "cookie-cutter" in appearance. If you must use the templates available in your accounting or business software, see if you can customize them with your logo, brand colors, and typography choices. Making minor layout revisions can help differentiate them.

It's always best to use company letterhead, business cards, and marketing collateral that have been professionally designed. Nothing looks worse than marketing collateral created in Microsoft Word with clip art and six font styles!

Develop and use a standardized e-mail signature template as part of your brand standards. This avoids the variety of signatures your employees may develop on their own. Flowery and overly colorful signatures, background wallpaper, and clip art are definitely unprofessional, as well as having no signature at all.

Ensure that you use a font size that e-mail recipients can easily read. If it's too small for a desktop computer, it'll be even harder to read on mobile devices. Use your company's typography style and colors for brand consistency.

Take into account that some people read their e-mails in text mode, so avoid using images in your signatures. Besides, you never know how recipients' servers will treat these messages. They can be blocked as SPAM.

Ensure you and your team use assigned company e-mail addresses — not those from Yahoo, AOL, Gmail, or Hotmail, which are unprofessional and raise doubts on the business' authenticity. Tying your e-mail address to your company's domain name is still the norm.

If you're primarily using mobile devices, set them up to receive business e-mails. It's more professional than using the mobile account as your sole contact address.

There's also some debate on using the mobile device signatures that default on many cell phones. "Sent from my iPhone" may appear pretentious or annoying. Instead, change the signature to one that is more professional. *PCMag* provides guidelines on changing the default.

Lastly, always spell check your templates and materials for grammatical and typographical errors. Sometimes, it's the simplest boo-boos that can make your brand look unprofessional.

CHOOSING THE "RIGHT" HIRES

When hiring new employees, you want to look for sharp-minded people who not only fit your company culture, but will present your brand with professionalism and excellence. They will control the customer experience, so it's crucial that they're invested, energetic, and empowered to make sound decisions on your company's behalf.

Since they will likely be the first brand touchpoint for your customers and clients, hire people with the right soft skills — positive attitudes, good interpersonal skills, outgoing personalities, enthusiasm, conversational strengths, warmth, an excellent command of the company's language of choice, and a desire to serve. They should ideally be open-minded, too, without prejudices or biases that can adversely affect customer relationships.

Candidates usually dress to impress during job interviews, so your first meeting with them may not be indicative of their daily attire. That's why asking for a shorter, second interview is a good idea to gain a second perspective.

When you're down to final candidates and you begin calling their work references, ask if their appearance, manners, and behaviors have been consistently professional. It's not a common question but one that has important implications for your company's brand reputation.

CHARACTERISTICS OF PROFESSIONAL EMPLOYEES

To give your small business an edge, here's a list of characteristics it can set as objectives for employee professionalism:

- accountable
- approachable
- collaborative
- communicative
- compassionate
- competent

- confident
- courteous
- customer focused
- flexible
- positive
- presentable
- proactive
- punctual
- reliable
- resourceful
- respectful
- responsible
- skilled and knowledgeable
- supportive
- willing to help

Small businesses often use professionalism to help them establish a good reputation in the business environment. Because many small businesses have limited capital resources during the early years of operations, an important advertising strategy is word-of-mouth. Small businesses that treat each customer in a professional manner and display a strong work ethic when completing business functions or responsibilities can help develop positive goodwill with consumers. (Osmond Vitez, "Meaning of Professionalism and Work Ethic," Demand Media, *Houston Chronicle*)

BE GRACIOUS WHEN THINGS GO WRONG

This is a biggie. One thing I've learned over time... things will definitely go wrong, no matter how much you work to avoid them. The key to small business marketing and branding success is how you professionally manage blunders.

Here's a real-life example that occurred with my own company. What would you have done?

One of our local clients asked us to edit, design, and print several brochures for an upcoming event. The designer who had been working on the project backed out and left the client scrambling. We stepped in to keep things on track.

We used the existing design framework to create the required collateral pieces and meet the client's timeframe. We allowed for more copy revisions than what was stipulated in our agreement and did one of the elements pro bono. The client was happy and his bosses were, too. Until...

During the course of shipping the printed brochures from our trade printer's plant to the client's office location, the shipper (a big brand international shipping company) lost the boxes. For five days!!

As soon as we found out, we kept in constant contact with our printer for updates on the lost boxes. In the meantime, the clock was ticking on the client's deadline and we were panicking.

Our print supplier agreed to reprint the brochures and ship them ASAP by air. We picked up the boxes at the airport and personally delivered them to the client's home within an hour of the flight's arrival. Phew. So we thought.

Throughout the delay, we assumed full responsibility, apologizing profusely, even though it was the shipping company's fault, not ours.

I advised the client that we would NOT charge him for the print job, which he appreciated. When the lost shipment finally arrived later that week, he was able to use the surplus quantity at no additional expense.

Being gracious and professional during mishaps like this can distinguish your small business from its competitors. Customers learn to count on you even when things go awry.

However, after a fiasco, there's no guarantee that you'll retain these customers. It's a crapshoot. A lot depends on the relationship history, whether there have been any previous mishaps, and whether clients are understanding.

All you can do is prevent errors to the best of your ability and repeat the same gracious and professional behavior when there are mess-ups. You'll be better able to sleep knowing you did everything you could while maintaining your composure, professionalism, and hopefully, your company's brand reputation.

10 GRACIOUS THINGS TO DO WHEN YOU HIT THOSE BUMPS IN THE ROAD

1. **Diffuse customers' panic, anger, or negativity by staying calm and listening.**

   If you panic (and you will at times), keep your customer communication even keeled, warm, and friendly. Empathize with customers while expressing your concerns, as long as it accompanies your plan to solve the problem ASAP.

2. **Keep customers informed regularly.**

    B2B customers have their own deadlines and internal people to please. Do everything you can to make your contacts look good and keep them apprised of any foreseeable problems. If you keep them in the dark, they will harbor negative feelings about you and your company.

    B2C customers also have personal deadlines. Keep them posted in the same manner.

3. **Jump through hoops to solve problems as quickly as you can.**

    The longer misfortunes stay active, the worse it gets for your customer relationship. It's straightforward.

4. **If the mishap is your doing, 'fess up.'**

    Take responsibility and tell customers that you will do whatever it takes to correct problems. Apologize.

5. **If problems belong to one of your suppliers or an external process, do the same thing.**

    Same as #4.

6. **Never blame someone in your own company.**

    Your company is ONE entity. Finger pointing is counterproductive, unprofessional, and damaging to your small business brand.

7. **Once you resolve incidents, send customers a letter, handwritten note, or personalized e-mail expressing your regret.**

For B2B customers, add a nice promotional product with it, a gift card, or something that they value. As an option, you can follow up with a phone call or e-mail a few days later to gauge their attitude towards your business. If no one replies, you may be out of luck for repeat business. It will depend on several factors.

For B2C customers, add a discount coupon with your note, an invitation to a special product launch, or a voucher for a free product or service.

8. **If you can, write off the cost.**

Depending on the severity of mistakes, refund or write off customers' purchases. If it's too costly and/or damaging to your company, offer a discount on the current invoice or a future purchase. Or ask customers how you can make it up to them. Sometimes, they simply want an apology.

9. **Don't keep throwing yourself at their mercy.**

If you're over apologizing, it can appear desperate. Once you've done all you can, keep in touch like you did before the incident. If they're on your e-mail or direct mail list, don't remove them. Carry on.

10. **Sometimes, time can heal the relationship if it's temporarily broken.**

These customers may replace you and return after dealing with another company. Or they may never return at all and you'll have to live with that.

Customers don't expect you to be perfect. They do expect you to fix things when they go wrong. (Donald Porter, CBE, former VP, British Airways, former chief manager of corporate communications, Lloyds Bank, quoted in Daily Business Quotes)

Being gracious and professional doesn't come naturally to some people, but with training and practice, anyone can learn this skill. Just remember how you want to be treated when you're the customer and you should be fine.

IDEA #4 TAKEAWAY

Running a small business professionally can certainly give it a business edge. From appearances, behaviors, ethics, and communications, each impression your company leaves with its employees and customers affects its brand reputation, credibility, customer confidence, level of trust, and ultimately, its ability to succeed.

IDEA #5

BE NIMBLE. BE QUICK.

The world is changing at a faster pace than at any other time in modern history. How some small businesses operated five or ten years ago can be impracticable today. Technology, innovation, and customer demand are constantly evolving. That's why it's important for your small business to stay abreast of its marketplace, marketing and business trends, and the general business climate.

Being nimble involves a combination of several characteristics: flexibility, open-mindedness, responsiveness, and competitiveness. Without these strengths, businesses run the risk of stagnating and becoming stale, sure signs that they will experience customer attrition.

The interesting aspect about nimbleness is that it may not necessarily incur a big expense, even when the results can have a huge impact. Take social media (SM) as an example.

Once it became clear that SM participation was not a passing fad, and that every business could benefit from it and customers expected it, many small businesses jumped on board. Hard costs are negligible. What it *does* take is an investment of time.

Companies that were quick and adapted early built their SM profiles and created followings that in many cases, enhanced their businesses over time. They recognized that this marketing communications channel was innovative and fresh, giving them direct access to their customers and prospects in ways they never had previously.

Additionally, creating and contributing content in multiple channels have boosted these companies' search engine optimization (SEO), increasing their presence in online search engines so more customers and prospects can find them.

The companies that waited, entered the fray after their competition had a stronger foothold, putting them at a disadvantage. Even worse were the businesses that still sat on the sidelines, waiting to participate altogether.

This lack of agility and forward thinking has more to do with attitude than cost. Doing things "the way we've always done it" is not a panacea for marketing and branding success.

It's true that some businesses cannot participate in SM marketing because of the nature of their industry or profession, or for security or privacy reasons. However, these companies are in the minority. For the vast majority, the advantages can certainly outweigh the disadvantages.

KEEP ON TOP OF THINGS

In order to maintain a nimble position, it's important to keep on top of new trends and innovations. In addition to attending conferences and ongoing training programs, you can read selective trade and business publications. From traditional trade and business magazines and newspapers, to digital publications, blogs, white papers, and marketing research studies, small businesses can learn what's coming down the pipeline and prepare.

Remember the character, Motel ("Mottle") the tailor, in the play and film *Fiddler on the Roof*? His big dream (besides marrying Tevye's daughter, Tzeitel) was to save enough money to buy a new invention – a sewing machine.

Motel had been reading about the sewing machine product launch, and since no other tailor in his geographic area had one, he knew it could change the nature of his business. Once he had his own machine, he could adopt the new technology, cut labor costs, keep on top of new trends and equipment, capture market share, and... make more money.

Today, many small businesses can market to larger geographic areas, if not globally, making the case for nimbleness even more crucial. Openness to change, agility, and quick adaptation can mean the difference between staying in business and growing, or losing market share and closing shop.

SMALL BUSINESSES CAN "TURN EASIER" THAN BIGGER ONES

Since the beginning of time, all life on our planet has evolved and adapted to changing environments in order to survive. The status quo does not exist, especially today.

Who could have imagined just 10 or 20 years ago that we'd be communicating with devices no bigger than the palms of our hands? As a child, I would have thought it science fiction, yet it is now the norm. Think of what is yet to come!

With our world changing so rapidly, small businesses have a distinct advantage for agility that larger companies and corporations don't always have. They can "turn" and adapt quicker, whereas bigger companies often have more difficulty in embracing change and responding to it.

Larger companies need more stakeholders to buy into any changes and innovations. Picture these businesses as freighters transporting goods across the oceans. Because of their size, it takes maneuvering and time to change course.

Now imagine that your small business is a rowboat with two oars for steering. You can turn on a dime in a few seconds.

Many small businesses, especially sole proprietorships, family-run operations, and home-based companies, have the flexibility to work during off hours to meet customer demands, close deals, and build their companies. They may be unsaddled with excessive equipment and physical stuff to weigh them down. Without high fixed costs like multiple salaries, rent, insurance, etc., their companies are also better able to adapt as conditions change.

Small businesses have fewer employees, making internal communication and decision making simpler. Building a cohesive company culture can be of great advantage when it comes to team building, embracing change, and adopting innovative approaches.

Nimble small businesses also have the flexibility to scale up or down as necessary. Hiring flexible employees with several talents and skills and using outsourced consultants and specialists can keep costs low.

Being prudent and monitoring expenses help small businesses remain solvent and deft, regardless of the economic trends or situations. Keeping an eye on internal trends and thresholds contributes to being proactive and not reactive.

This ability to make quick turns and modifications is a huge advantage. I believe that's why small businesses are getting more contracts and projects that previously went to larger companies. Customers have a more direct line to the people in charge — those who can make decisions and revisions easier and deliver with personalized customer service.

Speed, nimbleness and agility are some of the greatest pluses of small businesses. They can make decisions, rapidly implement them, closely monitor their progress and either amplify their efforts, if successful, or change direction if not. (Kevin Gilroy, "Agility At The Speed Of Small Business," *D!gitalist Magazine* by SAP)

SMALL BUSINESSES CAN TEST THE WATERS

Small business teams communicate more regularly, integrate their responsibilities more frequently, and know one another's capabilities better. If they experiment and fail, it can be less detrimental than for larger companies.

Using creative shoestring marketing and branding ideas can often bring better results than spending a lot on more traditional tools. Of course, there are no guarantees, and often luck plays a role, but there are many examples of small companies getting a big bang from tested creative campaigns that eventually went viral or gained national exposure.

SMALL BUSINESSES CAN EASILY COLLABORATE

When small businesses receive larger projects or orders, they may not have the capacity to deliver everything on their own. That's where collaboration with like-minded companies and partners can be of great benefit.

Can you imagine Coke and Pepsi working together on a new product? Highly unlikely. Yet two or more small companies can easily play together in the business sandbox without hurting their individual brands. In fact, collaboration may present more opportunities than working alone.

SHARE

Sharing your best practices and experiences with small business partners can help your company grow and build its brand reputation.

Here's a fictitious example:

A florist owner (Morgan) meets an event planner (Linda) at a local networking event. The conversation turns to IT service providers and how costs can add up for small companies. Morgan shares the name of his computer technician and vouches for his reliability and fair pricing.

Linda thanks Morgan for the referral and they both exchange business cards, agreeing to set up a lunch meeting. During their lunch, Linda tells Morgan that her regular florist is soon retiring and she's looking for a talented and reliable floral supplier. They make a match and both small businesses benefit from collaborating and making mutual referrals.

There are other ways to benefit from collaboration:

Rick's small consulting business has outgrown its home-based office; he wants to rent commercial space downtown but finds it too pricey.

He asks his network for referrals and discovers that Helen's elder care company has an unused office she's willing to rent. Until her company requires that space and while Rick's business grows, they will mutually benefit from the arrangement.

Another cost-saving example is when two or more noncompeting or complementary entrepreneurs or business owners agree to share office space and/or resources and staff to reduce costs. Sharing marketing expenses is another way to decrease overhead while building brand awareness.

Let's say there are seven different companies located in the same strip mall. Advertising separately in the local business publication would be cost prohibitive, but when they pool their resources, they can create one ad to market their products and services at the same location.

Collaboration can be less formal, too. An accountant recommends a lawyer. The lawyer puts in a good word for a corporate trainer. The corporate trainer endorses a local business meeting site. And so on...

SMALL BUSINESSES CAN TAKE MORE CALCULATED RISKS

Taking risks and making mistakes involve a learning process. Remaining stagnant and avoiding new opportunities aren't the best way to grow your business, unless you are perfectly content managing its current size.

When small businesses want to compete with the "bigger boys," they can take calculated risks to attract attention and customers. In case of failure, the brand fallout can be far less damaging to small companies than for corporations. And sometimes, no one will be the wiser.

The smartest action before taking any risks is to evaluate them properly beforehand. Consult your employees, small business partners, and others in your network to check if you've overlooked anything.

Take all scenarios into account. Prepare for the unexpected with backup plans and extra resources. You really never know how things will turn out, so be astute and cautious.

One of the worst-case scenarios of creative risk-taking occurred in 2007:

Turner Broadcasting contracted a small guerrilla marketing agency, Interference, Inc., to promote its new adult cartoon show called *Aqua Teen Hunger Force*.

The agency subcontracted two men to set out more than three dozen electronic light boards around Boston, depicting a middle-finger-waving moon man, a character in the show.

But the unexpected happened. The signs triggered repeated bomb scares and prompted closings at Boston University and bridges and boat traffic along a stretch of the Charles River.

What was originally a risk-taking, guerrilla campaign turned into a nightmare, even though critics claimed that Boston authorities overreacted. No one could have expected the fallout and negative PR, not to mention the $2 million settlement that Turner and Interference had to pay. (CNN, February 5, 2007)

Of course, this is an atypical example. On the flip side, in 2009, a virtual phone system provider called GotVMail rebranded itself under the company name of Grasshopper (Grasshopper.com).

When the small business wanted to build buzz about its new brand, the Grasshopper team launched a multisensory marketing campaign, sending unique direct mail pieces to 5,000 of the most influential politicians, business leaders, journalists, authors, and bloggers in the US and Canada. Each package included a link to an animated, kinetic typography video embedded on the company's landing page.

However, what received the most attention were the five 'real' chocolate-covered grasshoppers included in each package that reinforced the Grasshopper brand. Needless to say, the campaign was a huge success, scoring Grasshopper viral attention that solidified its rebranding and marketing campaign.

MAINTAINING A SMALL MENTALITY

Whether your small business decides to grow or remain small, it's important for it to maintain a "small" mentality in order to stay nimble and quick.

Remember the Avis tagline, "We try harder?" The company used that slogan for 50 years until 2012 when it changed to "It's Your Space," targeting busy business travelers. Trying harder makes an excellent mantra for small businesses that want to stand out and take advantage of new opportunities.

Here are some ideas to help maintain a small mentality:

- Weave a hungry attitude throughout the business culture. Becoming complacent as the company grows can spell disaster swiftly.

- Invest in, and focus on, customer relationships. The more personalized and amazing these relationships are, the better chances you have that they will stick around. This is one area where many growing and larger companies fail.

- Share your small business stories with customers. They can be endearing and spreadable.

- Make every brand touchpoint count. Being smaller means having more control over customer experiences.

- Try new things on a smaller level to test if they work. Enlist your customers and employees for feedback.

- Maintain your network of friends, colleagues, and partners. These are the people to whom you can turn for advice and guidance.

IDEA #5 TAKEAWAY

Small businesses have the distinct advantage of being nimbler and quicker than their larger counterparts. By keeping on top of trends, sharing and collaborating with other small businesses, taking calculated risks, and staying true to a customer-oriented mindset, your company can remain flexible, open-minded, responsive, and competitive. And more successful.

nimble and quick

IDEA #6

DEMONSTRATE SMALL BUSINESS SOCIAL RESPONSIBILITY (SBSR)

Small business social responsibility (SBSR) is the equivalent term I have given to this sector's practice of corporate social responsibility (CSR).

 **Corporate Social Responsibility:**
"A commitment to improve community well-being through discretionary business practices and contributions of corporate resources." (Philip Kotler and Nancy Lee, *Corporate Social Responsibility: Doing the Most Good for Your Company and Your Cause*, 2005)

I also like this explanation provided by the Harvard Kennedy School's Mossavar-Rahmani Center for Business and Government:

Corporate social responsibility encompasses not only what companies do with their profits, but also how they make them. It goes beyond philanthropy and compliance and addresses how companies manage their economic, social, and environmental impacts, as well as their relationships in all key spheres of influence: the workplace, the marketplace, the supply chain, the community, and the public policy realm.

When we look at recent studies, we see overwhelming data that demonstrate how customer affinity rises for socially responsible companies. So noted the *2015 Cone Communications/Ebiquity Global CSR Study*. Of the study's 9,000+ global consumers, respondents unequivocally believe that companies must operate responsibly to address social and environmental issues.

- A majority (91%) expect companies to do more than make a profit.

- 84% say whenever possible they try to purchase products or services that are socially or environmentally responsible.

- 90% would like to see more responsible products and services offered from companies.

- 88% expect companies to report on the progress of their CSR efforts, and nearly as many (86%) say if a company makes CSR commitments, it should be accountable for producing and communicating results.

Although a lot of data verify the benefits of social responsibility practices in enterprise B2C companies, there's been very little empirical data on B2B companies. However, in 2012, a University of Mannheim, Germany study discovered that CSR activities could also distinctly increase customer loyalty in a B2B environment.

What about your small business? Surely, CSR is reserved for the corporate sector, right?

Wrong. Small businesses have been involved in social responsibility long before the term "corporate social responsibility" was coined. They didn't necessarily broadcast their practices and did them for altruistic reasons, not realizing there were business advantages, too.

So whether your company is a sole proprietorship or has employees, it has much to gain by engaging in responsible business practices and getting involved in its local, regional, or national community. Not only is it beneficial for your business survival and brand, it's also good for your soul.

What does it take to survive? Aside from manic drive, moxie, hard work, creativity and luck ... *maybe a sense of connectedness to a community, local or more global.* (Tom Post, "The Surprising Secret Behind Small Business Success," *Forbes*)

BENEFITS OF PRACTICING SMALL BUSINESS SOCIAL RESPONSIBILITY

- Global consumers state they have a more positive image (93%), are more likely to trust (90%) and are more loyal to (88%) companies that support social and environmental issues. (*2015 Cone Communications/Ebiquity Global CSR Study*)

- 71% of global consumers would be willing to pay more for a socially and environmentally responsible product. (*2015 Cone Communications/Ebiquity Global CSR Study*)

- 62% of global consumers would choose to work for a socially responsible company, even if the salary would be less than at other companies. (*2015 Cone Communications/Ebiquity Global CSR Study*)

- Companies where corporate citizenship is integrated are 2.2 times more likely to access new markets and 2.3 times more likely to retain employees. (*State of Corporate Citizenship 2014*, Boston College, Carroll School of Management Center for Corporate Citizenship)

- Companies dedicated to at least 4 years of corporate citizenship are 3 times more likely to improve risk management and 3.9 times more likely to reduce employee health costs. (*State of Corporate Citizenship 2014*, Boston College, Carroll School of Management Center for Corporate Citizenship)

Small business social responsibility can:

- attract, retain, and motivate employees while engaging them in SBSR activities
- enhance the company's brand reputation as a good "corporate" citizen
- promote customer and brand loyalty
- increase customers and sales
- save money (recycling, turning off power, retaining employees)
- expand the company's visibility in the community
- provide good stories and content to share with target audiences
- build up competitive advantage
- foster greater public trust

For a larger view of the infographic (in color), visit:
http://elainefogel.com/sbsr-infographic.jpg

WAYS TO PRACTICE SBSR

There are many ways your small business can practice SBSR. You can choose one or two and do them really well, or decide to tackle several. I suggest you enlist your employees' input before engaging in an SBSR program, as their involvement is vital to your program's success. If your business is a sole proprietorship, then it's totally up to you where you want to focus.

First, let's examine each component of social responsibility. Some are optional while others represent basic or legislated business practices.

EMPLOYEE MANAGEMENT

Employment and Labor Standards

First, your business, regardless of its size, must comply with regulations established by the US Department of Labor. In Canada, laws are set by the Canadian Government's Labour Program. You need to check your state or provincial regulations as well.

Labor laws legislate things like wages, overtime pay, severance, vacation, recordkeeping, employment and pay equity, disability issues, health and safety, health benefits, retirement standards, worker's compensation, worker protection, child labor protection, work authorizations, and labor relations, among others.

Compliance with these laws is every business owner's responsibility and affects a company's brand reputation if something goes awry and it becomes public knowledge. As we discussed in Idea #2, respecting and taking care of your employees and ensuring their health, safety, and satisfaction are part of your small business' brand.

Professional Development

Working for a small business has both advantages and disadvantages over working in the corporate sector. Many small businesses have some limitations in what they can provide to employees. Yet your business will benefit greatly and demonstrate SBSR when it offers professional development opportunities to its employees. Not only do employees appreciate additional skills training, they tend to stay on the job longer and are more loyal to the company.

Professional development activities can range from providing in-house training materials to attending conferences. Here are some ideas for your company:

- Host lunch-and-learn workshops with guests from your industry/profession or in-house experts.

- Subsidize, or pay fully for, work-related courses at a local college, university, or association.

- Purchase webinars and online courses for employees.

- Develop a work library of relevant books, DVDs, and trade magazines your employees can borrow.

- Join a local chamber of commerce or professional/ trade association and invite employees to lectures and presentations of interest.

Enabling employees to grow professionally sends a positive message that your business cares about them and is sharing responsibility for their career advancement.

BUSINESS OPERATIONS

Although small businesses are not required to comply with the same set of regulations that public ones do, using ethical and responsible business practices can certainly affect their brand reputations. These should be woven into the core of daily functions and company values.

Risk Management

As part of running a small business, and depending on its size, scope, and location, it's valuable to develop procedures and plans for all business operations. To mitigate risks, regularly assess things like security, property, emergency and disaster plans, compliance issues, mechanisms, environments, vehicle and machinery operation, technology, knowledge, supply chain, finances, reputation, product or service delivery, etc.

Aside from improving processes:

This part of your small business social responsibility creates an insurance-like firm asset and protects the firm from drastic turbulence during financial downturns. (Wenbin Sun, PhD)

Transparency and Trust

Unlike public companies that file regular financial statements and reports, your small business isn't accountable to anyone but its principals and/or investors - if there are any. However, practicing transparency with employees, customers, and suppliers can definitely help cultivate and sustain relationships of trust. When people believe in your small business, its brand reputation grows.

This doesn't require you to share confidential information with stakeholders. But by communicating any upcoming changes, product or service adjustments, and strategic decisions that will affect them, you can help allay their fears and anxieties. Give them opportunities to participate in business-related discussions and contribute to a positive work environment.

Ethical Behavior

Small business customers may not always ask about a company's internal behaviors. But if they care about social, environmental, and other ethical issues, which many do, discovering bad behavior can certainly send them running.

Employees will see through wrongdoing very quickly. They'll tell others and staff turnover will be higher than average. Not only does this situation have a hard cost to any small business, it can easily erode its brand as well.

What does unethical behavior entail? It can be as seemingly innocuous as stealing office supplies to major offenses such as:

- accepting and not recording cash payments
- treating employees poorly
- placing used or refurbished goods back into inventory without identifying them or marking them down
- paying temporary workers in cash and not recording it or submitting appropriate taxes
- dumping waste in illegal sites
- cheating customers, suppliers, or employees
- not honoring contracts or agreements
- resorting to misleading advertisements or marketing practices

A 2014 study entitled, "The Slippery Slope: How Small Ethical Transgressions Pave The Way For Larger Future Transgressions," reported by The Huffington Post, demonstrates that stealing a pen from your office could find yourself on a path toward becoming the next Bernie Madoff.

According to the study, which was published in the Journal of Applied Psychology, minor unethical behavior at work, if undetected, puts workers on a "slippery slope" that could lead to worse behavior over time. (Emily Cohn, "Stealing A Pen At Work Could Turn You On To Much Bigger Crimes," *The Huffinton Post*, June 26, 2014)

To ensure that your small business maintains a solid brand reputation, it should make ethical business practices part of its values, procedures, and standards and regularly reinforce them with employees. Stakeholders will feel more secure and trusting, knowing that they are in good hands.

ENVIRONMENT

Environmental concerns have been at the forefront of the business sector and public interest for many years. People want to know whether companies are good citizens or are contributing to unhealthy conditions that can affect their communities.

Even though situations have improved drastically over the past decade or so, human-caused environmental disasters occur all the time. Some are huge like the 2010 BP oil spill in the Gulf of Mexico, while others may happen on a reduced scale, committed by smaller companies.

An example is when 233,000 gallons of molasses accidentally spilled into Hawaii's Honolulu Harbor near

Sand Island in September 2013. Because molasses sucks up all the available oxygen in the water, it caused fish and other sea life to suffocate.

Our environments are also affected by natural disasters and weather patterns such as tornadoes, hurricanes, and fires. Although humans are the victims, not the perpetrators of these calamities, weather can have an adverse impact on millions of people.

A good example is the series of snowstorms during the 2014-2015 winter that paralyzed the midwest and northeast of North America. These hostile weather patterns took a toll on many companies' supply chains, product deliveries, profits, and brand reputations, regardless of their sizes.

As global climates change, there are growing concerns about their effects on our health. According to Gallup's annual environment survey (2015), Americans express greatest concern over more proximate threats including pollution of drinking water, as well as pollution of rivers, lakes and reservoirs, and air pollution.

So where do small businesses fit into this grand scheme of environmental responsibility?

For one, small companies must comply with environmental laws. Otherwise, whether unwittingly or intentionally, the consequences can include fines, business shut downs, or criminal charges, any of which can harm their brands.

Check the regulations at the US Environmental Protection Agency (EPA) where you can access its Small Entity Compliance Guides online to know your obligations. In Canada, Environment Canada oversees regulations.

Other initiatives of your small business that exemplify its commitment to protecting and preserving the environment include:

Water Conservation

Periodically check faucets for leaks and repair them. Encourage employees to turn off faucets thoroughly so they don't drip.

When purchasing appliances, toilets, or equipment, look for water-efficient models. They may cost a few more bucks upfront, but you should be able to recoup that with water savings.

If your company has external equipment, try reducing the frequency of cleaning it. Sweep external areas instead of using a water hose.

Many government resources on this topic are available for businesses and industries.

Fuel Conservation

If your small business operates any vehicles, buy fuel-efficient or hybrid cars and trucks if possible. To improve gas mileage, remove unneeded items that add weight.

Keep company vehicle tires properly inflated to recommended pressures. This can greatly decrease fuel consumption.

Discourage employees from driving over posted speed limits. Not only does it prevent traffic violations, it saves on gasoline.

Outfit company vehicles with global positioning systems (GPS) or ask employees to use their mobile GPS apps, to encourage taking alternative routes during rush hour or slowdowns. Idling in traffic is a killer for fuel consumption.

Electricity Conservation

Encourage employees to turn off lights, computers, monitors, and equipment overnight and on weekends. If security is a concern, install a system with motion detectors.

Put any outdoor illuminated signs on timers so they're off during the day and off hours. Use energy-efficient light bulbs and regularly clean them to eliminate the dust and grime that accumulate. Dirty lighting means reduced brightness.

If you have control of your company's electric heat and air conditioning, program temperatures a degree or two below or above the 'norms,' respectively. Every degree change from recommended temperatures can reduce energy use. In the summer, use ceiling fans or portable rotating fans to make it feel cooler.

Keep equipment condenser or evaporator coils clean and replace filters as needed.

Waste Reduction

Foam and Plastic

Use and wash ceramic, stone, porcelain, or glass mugs and dishes instead of those made from polystyrene foam or plastic. These latter materials don't break down easily and create too much litter on our streets. Another alternative is to use items made mostly of recycled materials.

A big environmental culprit is plastic. Plastic bottles and bags create the most widespread form of pollution on beaches and in oceans. The average American throws away approximately 185 pounds of plastic per year! The Great Pacific Garbage Patch is located in the North Pacific Gyre off the coast of California and is the largest ocean garbage site in the world. This floating mass of plastic is twice the size of Texas, with plastic pieces outnumbering sea life six to one. (Lynn Hasselberger, "22 Preposterous Facts about Plastic Pollution," *EcoWatch*, April 7, 2014)

There are a few alternatives for small businesses that have several employees:

Consider placing a water fountain in the office or adding a filtration system to the kitchen faucet. You can also contract with a water cooler supplier that delivers large reusable bottles of water on a regular schedule. Or simply ask employees to bring their own ecofriendly, reusable water bottles to work.

Ask employees to replace sandwich bags and juice cartons with reusable lunch bags or boxes that include reusable plastic bottles. Encourage them to use reusable bags at work. Better yet, order reusable bags imprinted with your company logo and give them away to the staff and customers.

Paper

Another way to reduce waste is to turn used paper, envelopes, and outdated forms and stationery into scratch paper. As long as documents aren't confidential and the print is on one side of the paper, the reverse side is available for note taking. Use a paper cutter to halve or quarter letter-sized paper and store in small bins or empty corrugated boxes.

Copier and Printer Cartridges

If it's possible, refill the toner or ink cartridges on your copy machine and printer. If not, return them to the nearest office store for loyalty rewards credit.

Coffee Filters

If you have coffeemakers in the office, buy reusable filters instead of paper ones to save money and reduce waste.

Cleaning Supplies

Use refillable bottles for cleaning products and bathroom soap dispensers. Check labels for formulas that are environmentally friendly.

Instead of using paper towels in the restrooms, use a refillable, rolling cloth towel dispenser or automatic, wall-mounted drying machines.

Packaging

Buy office supplies in bulk with minimal packaging. Individually wrapped items create more waste.

Check with your suppliers to see if they can reuse the cardboard boxes and foam pellets they use to ship goods to your business.

Metals, Wood, and Concrete

If your small business uses metals, concrete, or wood, unused remnants can be recycled or sold. Check with government agencies for more information.

Your company can truly exemplify social responsibility for the environment by practicing conservation and reducing waste. Convey your commitment and its brand reputation will benefit.

COMMUNITY CONNECTIONS

There are countless ways your small business can get involved with its local communities as part of SBSR efforts.

COMMUNITY HEROES

Benefits of Connecting With Your Communities

There are many benefits to connecting with your community. From a business perspective, here's what it can do:

- Increase your business' brand awareness and recognition with target audiences.

- Enhance your company's image and brand reputation.

- Build and boost customer loyalty.

- Increase word-of-mouth (WOM) referrals and build buzz.

- Promote trust for your business.

- Reduce marketing and customer acquisition costs.

- Increase leads, prospects, and sales.

- Reduce complaints.

- Improve employee recruitment, engagement, commitment, and retention.

- Reduce risk.

- Expand your company's contacts and networks.

- Improve your business' competitiveness and market position.

Ways to Connect With Your Community

From volunteering and charitable donations to cause marketing and advocacy, here are some ideas for your consideration:

Sponsorship

Sponsorship enables your small business to provide financial support for a community program, project, or charitable cause. In addition to reaching new customers and gaining WOM buzz, you can meet and network with bigger sponsors. Some of these larger companies partner with small businesses, so being front and center can't hurt.

If your company has the funds to do this, it can enhance its image and gain exposure while establishing goodwill in the communities it serves. Some sponsorship opportunities include:

- amateur sports team uniforms

- new playground or equipment for the local school or community

- school and nonprofit fundraising events such as dinners, yard sales, runs, and walks

- small business trade shows and exhibits

- community celebrations such as Independence Day/ Canada Day picnics, and festivals

- association lunches and speaker series

- community arts events such as theatre and concerts

Some words of advice:

- Get sponsorship terms in writing, with expected deliverables for both parties. Then ensure your business meets the expectations.

- Abide by the established sponsorship rules and regulations. If you're unsure, ask before making assumptions. You don't want to get a bad reputation with event organizers.

Volunteering

Volunteering is good for us! A 2013 UnitedHealth Group study claimed that 76% of US adults who volunteered said that volunteering made them feel physically healthier and 78% reported that volunteering lowered levels of stress, both of which resulted in feeling better than adults who did not volunteer.

The study also indicated that compared to nonvolunteers, volunteers had better emotional well-being, including personal independence, capacity for rich interpersonal relationships, overall satisfaction with life, and improved mood and self-esteem.

The benefits for employers were many, too. Employees who volunteered brought more refined job skills to the workplace, had stronger people and teamwork skills, and effective time management skills.

Of those who volunteered together with work colleagues, 64% said that volunteering had strengthened these relationships and 80% claimed feeling better about their employer because of the employer's involvement in volunteer activities.

Employee volunteerism programs can help increase engagement and morale while helping a company become an active participant in its community – whether that be a local town or a global network. Not only do volunteerism programs help employers ensure their employees are happy and productive, they make the world a better place. (Anne Kreuser, "Boosting Employee Engagement Through Volunteerism," Edelman goodpurpose®)

If you are a sole proprietor, you may reap the same benefits when volunteering in your community. Additionally, you'll meet new people – some of whom may fall within your target audiences, while others can contribute to WOM referrals and your business' brand reputation.

If your small business has employees, it's advantageous to support their volunteer efforts or take a leadership role in developing a company volunteer program. Remember that a majority (93%) of US consumers said that they had a more positive image of companies that supported causes.

The facts are clear: promoting and providing employees with meaningful volunteer opportunities helps to attract top talent; engage, develop, and retain employees; boost public image; and improve the bottom line. (Michael Haberman, "Why Volunteering Is Good for your Business," *Huffington Post*, September 5, 2012)

Setting up an employee volunteer program takes some thought and strategy. Before developing a plan, ask employees for their input. They'll be much more invested when they have a say in selecting the cause or project.

According to my colleague, Rachel Hutchisson of Blackbaud's "Business Doing Good" initiative, most businesses with grassroots volunteer programs fall into three main categories:

1. **Company-sponsored service days**
   These projects, typically spearheaded by local nonprofits or umbrella groups like the United Way, give employees the opportunity to join in community-wide efforts. These events can be big, inspirational, and lots of fun.

2. **Team-building events**
   A team of your company's employees partners with a local nonprofit on projects that achieve two goals: build team unity and give back to the community.

3. **Individual service**
   Hutchisson's claim that individual volunteer service during work hours wasn't as prevalent as team activities was confirmed in the *2013 Employee Benefits Report* by the Society for Human Resource Management (SHRM). Only 20% of the respondents said they offered employees paid time off for volunteering and 18% offered paid time off to serve on the board of a community group or professional association.

However, this trend might be changing. SHRM's *2014 Future Insights* indicated that employers would adopt CSRS (corporate social responsibility and sustainability) and support employees' participation in these initiatives in order to compete for and retain top talent. Hopefully, we'd see volunteering increase, which might have a trickle-down effect on SBSR.

One key to a successful volunteer program is to make it fun and rewarding. Getting out of the office for a day or a few hours gives employees a break and an opportunity to do something different.

Make sure your company or the host agency provides refreshments and/or lunch to your employees. Periodically, organize award ceremonies to celebrate your company's community service efforts or create an incentive program with prizes for those who participate.

Hutchisson advises, "Highlight employees and teams that volunteer, showing that the company values their service to the community. Include photos of teams in action in your company newsletter, on bulletin boards in the office or on your website. Share the news with your employees, the community and your customers. People like to work with, buy from, and be connected to those who do good."

You can download Blackbaud's "Creating an Employee Volunteer Program at Your Small Business" at the link provided in the Resources section or by doing a keyword search online. It is chock-full of valuable information.

Here are some resources to help you find local volunteer opportunities:

- All for Good
- HandsOn Volunteer Action Centers
- idealist
- National Volunteer Week
- VolunteerMatch.org
- Volunteers of America

In Canada, visit Charity Village for volunteer opportunities.

Sharing Expertise

If your expertise can help others in your community, why not share it? A good way to "give back" is to offer a free event or seminar to those who can benefit from your knowledge. You or another company representative can do a presentation at a local service club, library, community center, or professional or trade association meeting.

If public speaking isn't your thing, consider mentoring an entrepreneur who's starting out in business or a professional who would welcome your guidance. You can consider youth mentorship programs as well.

Here are some resources to get you started:

In the US:

- MicroMentor by MercyCorps

- government-sponsored mentor organizations such as *SCORE*, Small Business Development Centers, and Women's Business Centers sponsored by the US Small Business Administration

- small business associations

- chambers of commerce

- alumni associations

- Junior Achievement

In Canada:

- Futurpreneur Canada

- Aboriginal Business Mentorship Program from the Canadian Council for Aboriginal Business

- AIM Foundation of Canada is a nonprofit developing and delivering youth mentor programs in Canada

- Getinvolved!, operated by the public television network TVO, has thousands of volunteer opportunities posted online

- You can also check state/provincial government websites to search for small business resources

Another avenue is to volunteer your business skills to a charity of your choice. Contact individual organizations directly and ask if they have a volunteer coordinator with whom you can discuss your desire to volunteer. Or check their websites for volunteer postings. Some have online volunteer forms you can complete and submit.

Another resource is a website called Catchafire, where nonprofits post their project needs in a variety of disciplines including accounting, branding, business development, database management, finance, fundraising, human resources, IT, legal services, photography, and marketing.

One thing to note... the value of your labor is not tax deductible in the US, but you can deduct incurred expenses related to them, such as supplies and car expenses. You can access this information at the IRS website.

In Canada, qualified charities can reimburse volunteers for their volunteer expenses and later accept payment returns as gifts, provided that volunteers return the amounts voluntarily. If volunteers have a right to reimbursement from registered charities for the expenses they incur, charities may treat the right to reimbursement as a gift in kind and issue a receipt for income tax purposes. Check the Canada Revenue Agency (CRA) site for more information.

Charitable Contributions

There are many ways your small business can contribute to community organizations. Options include cash donations, gifts of property, donor-advised funds, gifts in kind (such as products, services, and consulting), vehicle donations, and furniture and equipment that your business no longer needs.

If you want to have a more significant impact, smaller nonprofits would gladly welcome your support. Because they lack the larger organizations' resources, some may not have online giving portals and prefer checks to avoid credit card processing fees.

If you're looking for convenience and want to make all your company donations in one fell swoop, several websites are dedicated to this. Here are some examples:

- GivingTuesday is a national day of giving to kick off the holiday donating season. In addition to the US, this initiative includes six participating countries.

- JustGive.org

- NetworkforGood

In Canada, visit CanadaHelps.org.

Please note that if you want to gain a tax benefit at the same time as doing good, check with your tax advisor to ensure your specific contributions qualify for deductions. In Canada, check the CRA site to calculate your charitable tax credits.

Employee, Customer, and Supplier Giving and Engagement Campaigns

There are several ways your small business can engage employees, customers, and suppliers to join forces for charitable causes in the community.

Automatic employee payroll deductions are optional employer-coordinated programs that allow employees to authorize contributions to their charities of choice. If your business contracts with a payroll services company, ask if it has a charitable contributions option for paycheck deductions.

One of the oldest employee-giving campaigns is coordinated by United Way. This nonprofit organization, which operates in 41 countries and territories, has turnkey giving solutions that support its member agencies. Contact your local United Way for more information.

Company fundraising campaigns give small businesses opportunities to coordinate their own fundraising efforts. A few examples of these 'third-party' fundraising campaigns include fun events such as car washes, golf tournaments, book or bake sales, bowl-a-thons, Blue Jean Days, and rummage sales. Your company can gain more traction by inviting customers, suppliers, and employees' families to participate, when appropriate.

When you engage employees in the selection, planning, and implementation of fundraising events, they are more enthusiastic and invested in the outcome. Don't forget to take photos and use them on your website, in customer newsletters, and post-event news releases.

Fundraising portals offer small businesses the tools to engage employees, customers, suppliers, and social media "friends" in their charitable campaigns.

Here are some fundraising portal sites:

- Causes facilitates your company's efforts by supporting and organizing campaigns that impact its community.

- Causecast offers your business a centralized solution for volunteering, giving, matching, and rewarding.

- FirstGiving (a subsidiary of FrontStream) helps you set up your own grassroots fundraising page. It also provides a Donation Button Creator tool so you can create a customized button to raise funds for your charity of choice on your website, blog, or Facebook page. http://donatetab.firstgiving.com

- MyCharityofChoice assists individuals and groups in setting up fundraising campaigns.

- Razoo enables you to donate or fundraise for the causes your business cares about the most.

Cause Marketing

Cause marketing is one of the more successful and older methods that businesses have used to practice social responsibility. These programs represent strategic and mutually beneficial relationships between nonprofit organizations and businesses.

Nonprofits benefit by advancing their missions through association and partnership with recognized businesses, without investing their own limited resources. Businesses benefit by raising brand awareness, enhancing their brand reputations, attracting new customers, connecting with Millennials (who are socially conscious), demonstrating social responsibility, boosting customer interest in and loyalty to their products or services, and increasing sales. To review current statistics and learn how advantageous cause marketing can be, visit the Cause Marketing Forum.

A corporate example of cause marketing is the "Save Lids to Save Lives" promotion that Yoplait runs annually to support Susan G. Komen for the Cure. For every pink yogurt lid people send in, Yoplait donates 10¢ to the organization, up to a maximum of $2 million. This same principle can easily apply to small companies on a reduced scale.

I have yet to find ubiquitously accepted explanations for the existing types of cause marketing programs. So with the help of a few experts I admire, here are descriptions of the various types:

Cause-Related Marketing

Cause-related marketing was the original term used before "cause marketing" became more common. According to Kotler and Lee, in their book *Corporate Social Responsibility* (2005), cause-related marketing is when businesses make a contribution or donate a percentage of revenues to a specific cause [or charity] based on product [or service] sales.

Your small business can run a cause-related marketing campaign for a day or a longer period of time. Once a charity partner is in place, ensure you have a written agreement outlining deliverables and expectations for both parties.

It's also quite common for companies to pledge a minimum donation amount should their campaigns produce less than anticipated revenue in the start-up phase. You can negotiate with your charity of choice on the amount.

For small businesses without big marketing budgets to promote these campaigns, it may take some time to gain traction, but over time, your customers will come to expect and support them.

Purchase Plus

Purchase plus cause marketing is a campaign that B2C companies employ at points of sale. Employees can ask customers for donations using their charity partners' donation boxes or coin cans. Or they can ask if customers want to 'top up' their purchases by adding donations to cash register entries.

Frequently, companies will thank participating customers by placing their names on displays, adding a visual reminder of the business' social responsibility efforts. Purchase plus programs are low risk, making them viable options for small businesses.

Social Marketing

Social marketing is often confused with social media marketing; however, they are entirely different.

 **Social Marketing:**

"The use of commercial marketing principles and techniques to promote the adoption of a behavior that will improve the health or well-being of the target audience or of society as a whole." (Nedra Kline Weinreich, *Hands-On Social Marketing: A Step-by-Step Guide to Designing Change for Good*, 2011)

Typically, nonprofit organizations and government agencies partake in social marketing campaigns. Examples of some issues include smoking cessation, childhood obesity, recycling, and immunization.

Small businesses that want to raise funds for a specific issue should align themselves with a charitable organization focused on it. Customers may be leery of donating to an issue without knowing exactly where the money goes.

Licensing

Licensing is when businesses pay fees to nonprofit organizations for the rights to use their logos, trademarks, or other brand assets. These licensing agreements typically stipulate where brand assets can be applied, such as on products, marketing collateral, tags, or labels.

This type of cause marketing practice is more prevalent in the corporate sector. Realistically, licensing fees are too costly for most small businesses.

Cause Promotions

Cause promotions are marketing communication messages that businesses use to raise awareness and/ or support for a social issue, cause, or specific charity. Strategically aligned with a business' products and/ or services, they can build goodwill, demonstrate social responsibility, and boost customer interest and loyalty.

Examples of social issues include childhood obesity, effects of secondhand smoking, or climate change. Others can include specific diseases, recent disasters, hunger, or homelessness.

The last type of cause promotions involves communications that support specific local, regional, national, and international charitable organizations. For example, if a business wants to support hurricane relief efforts, it can select and promote the Red Cross as its charity of choice.

Before social media existed, businesses entered into partnership agreements with these charities. This enabled nonprofits to manage and control their brand assets and messaging while businesses benefited from the organizations' internal resources. These partnerships typically involved charitable contributions as well.

With social media prominently in the picture, cause promotions for specific charities have taken on an entirely new life. Individuals can easily become brand ambassadors for their favorite charities, promoting them to their social networks.

Small businesses can get in on the act, too, and post links to a charity's event landing pages, fundraising campaign microsites, and online stores year round or during short-term campaigns. These cause promotions are informal and either random or strategic in nature. Most charities welcome the added exposure and support.

However, if your small business wants to extend its charitable support with targeted campaigns that include both offline and online promotions, it would be wise to meet with the charity's senior leadership to develop a more formal partnership. This approach helps both parties manage their risks and ensures consistency in the charity's messaging, positioning, and branding.

SBSR TIPS

Be genuine in your small business social responsibility (SBSR) efforts. People will see through any phony gestures and more harm than good can come to a company's brand.

Be strategic when planning any SBSR campaigns. Ensure you can link them to your business' mission and core purpose, as well as your employees' values. Enlist employees to develop a plan collaboratively.

Don't worry about competing with corporations and larger companies. It's not a contest. Do what is feasible and manageable for your small business.

Start small, measure, and make adjustments along the way before biting off too much at a time.

IDEA #6 TAKEAWAY

Making small and gradual changes to your company's employee management policies, business operations, environmental stewardship, and community involvement can pay off big time. Practice social responsibility with heart, and your small business will be well on its way to success.

social responsibility

IDEA #7

BE STRATEGIC

First, let's define "strategy." Most of us use this word without a second thought. Yet how many know its meaning and the difference between strategy and "tactics?" Don't feel badly if you can't define them. I've read articles and posts by professional marketers who confuse the two terms.

In a nutshell, strategy is the plan and tactics are the actions you take to implement the plan. Pretty simple, isn't it?

Next, strategy *always* comes before tactics. Otherwise, it's like driving on the highway without knowing your destination. That would be a big waste of time and gas. Yet so many small business owners and professionals operate exactly like this! They are "doing" tactics without identifying where they're going. Many spend time, effort, and money on activities they think they should do.

Maybe they attended a small business seminar on social media marketing, so they're focusing on it. Or perhaps they read an article on blogging and decided to start a blog. But this reactive marketing activity isn't time or cost effective without a bona fide strategy.

If this tendency describes you and your small business, don't fret – chances are that you're about to change your mindset! I'll share a sensible approach to help you avoid spinning your wheels on activities that you assume will work; instead, you can do the due diligence and invest in what has a good chance of working.

Example:

In one of the strategic marketing communications workshops I facilitated, one participant expressed a desire to learn more about using social media marketing. She was convinced that it would help her organization achieve its objectives.

After going through the marketing communications planning process, she discovered that her target audiences were neither getting their information from social media nor participating in it. In fact, many of her target audiences had lower incomes or were retired, living in rural America, where broadband access is less ubiquitous and fewer people have easy access to computers.

Had she put all her efforts into social media marketing, she would have wasted her time and limited resources. Instead, she researched her audiences more thoroughly to learn where they got their information. That's when she developed a more suitable strategy.

Before we go further, I recommend deciding whether you want to tackle the plan yourself or seek professional assistance. Realistically, if you lack the time, inclination, or desire to work on the plan yourself and you have the financial resources, I suggest hiring an experienced marketing consultant to develop the plan with you.

This is especially valuable if your business is in startup mode. Contract with a professional who can help you create a business plan with a marketing and branding strategy as a subset. However, if paying for professional assistance isn't feasible and you want to develop a new plan or improve or update an old one, then let's continue.

Since the marketing and branding strategy is so important to your small business' success, I've included the framework for a full plan. I toyed with the notion of condensing or simplifying it as many other small business resources have done, but decided against it.

I believe that you should have the option to apply the strategy in its entirety or alternatively, decide which parts are essential for your specific business, which are less applicable, and what you want to delay or skip altogether. As such, Idea #7 is quite substantive, so I'll break it down into manageable chunks.

I recommend reading through it first to get the gist of the content and format before taking any action. If you tend to start projects enthusiastically and lose steam later, I encourage you to stay the course! Take it one step at a time so it's not overwhelming. Make the commitment now that you won't revert to your previous tactics without completing the strategy. Believe me; it will be worth the effort.

By the end of this exercise, you'll have captured where your company stands now, its overall business objectives, ideal customers and referral sources, brand characteristics, marketing and branding activities (tactics), and the measurement tools you'll need to identify what's working and what's not.

Accordingly, I've divided Idea #7 into four parts:

I. Market & Situation Analysis – your current marketplace and business position

II. Marketing & Branding Strategy – your business objectives and how to reach them

III. Marketing & Branding Tactics – your business actions to reach strategic objectives

IV. Metrics – measurement methods to determine which tactics are working or not

The final plan will read like a business report, with a cover page, table of contents, and the four sections. You'll be able to refer to the document regularly and share it with any outsourced marketing professionals.

Let's begin.

MARKETING & BRANDING PLAN COVER PAGE

- Company logo

- Marketing & Branding Plan for [name of your business]

- Company address and contact information

- Date (of plan completion)

TABLE OF CONTENTS

EXECUTIVE SUMMARY

Complete the entire plan first before writing the executive summary. You can then summarize the completed marketing and branding plan in one to two pages. The executive summary serves as the condensed version you can share with employees and other invested parties.

I. MARKET & SITUATION ANALYSIS

Whether your business is a startup or has existed for some time, a market and situation analysis describes where the marketplace and your company stand now. It also identifies your business objectives and any external trends and facts that affect the company. This part sets the foundation for your marketing and branding plan.

I-1) COMPANY OBJECTIVES

State the business' mission and vision.

- Mission statement: states why the company exists or what it is trying to accomplish.

  Example: "To bring inspiration and innovation to every athlete in the world." (Nike)

- Vision statement: states what things will look like in the future.

  Example: "Our vision is to be earth's most customer centric company; to build a place where people can come to find and discover anything they might want to buy online." (Amazon)

- List the company's business objectives. Some examples include: growth in company revenues and earnings, surpassing competition, increasing employee retention, or improving customer service.

I-2) COMPANY ANALYSIS

In paragraph format:

- Identify your company's current structure (sole proprietorship, LLC, or corporation).

- Identify which geographic area/s it primarily serves.

- State the company's business model. Is it a franchise, distributorship, retailer, wholesaler, e-commerce provider, manufacturer, or in direct sales?

- Provide a brief company background or history.

- Briefly describe the company's product and/or service offerings, capabilities, and core competencies.

I-3) SWOT ANALYSIS

A SWOT analysis identifies the strengths, weaknesses, opportunities, and threats to your business. Enlist input from your employees (if you have them) and select insiders. They will bring different perspectives that you need to know.

The easiest way to conduct this is to hold a strategy meeting as a group. Set up flipcharts and brainstorm until you've exhausted each list in the four categories. If you are a sole practitioner, ask your family and friends to participate.

It's important to include as much information as you can to fully evaluate your situation. Review all company areas and be as honest as possible. This is not the place to hide the negatives. Embracing them will show a more realistic picture and enable you to plan for them.

Strengths

Examine applicable, internal business areas for positives, including finance, human resources, technology, operations, manufacturing, sales and marketing, management, structure, and company culture. What does your company do well? What are its best assets? What are its competitive advantages?

Examples:

- "Our staff turnover rate has been reduced by 5% as a result of our new staff appreciation policies."

- "We have a long history and a positive reputation in this community."

Weaknesses

List weaknesses or specific aspects that need improvement.
Examples:

- "Our technology hardware is old and is impeding our ability to progress."

- "We haven't been able to increase staff salaries in three years."

Opportunities

Taking an external perspective, identify the existing elements that could present excellent opportunities for your small business.
Examples:

- "The local community college [name] has indicated an interest in working with us as a student co-op partner, possibly expanding the number of interns we can tap into for assistance."

- "If we offer more budget-conscious products, we can increase revenue."

Threats

Determine the external situations or factors that can have a detrimental effect on your business.
Examples:

- "Our largest competitor [name] has announced plans to add a location in our immediate vacinity."

- "The government is implementing an increase in minimum wage, affecting what we pay our new hires."

At this point, I would be remiss if I didn't mention an alternative to the SWOT analysis. Some critics believe that highlighting weaknesses and threats dwells on the negative and are not helpful in looking forward.

This other method is called SOAR and focuses on strengths, opportunities, aspirations, and results. This approach uses the process of "appreciative inquiry," which emphasizes the positive – what people or organizations do well – identifying their potential.

Appreciative Inquiry:

"Attempts to use ways of asking questions and envisioning the future in order to foster positive relationships and build on the present potential of a given person, organization or situation." (*Wikipedia*)

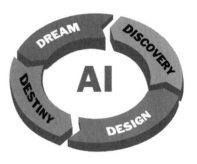

Rather than feeling hampered by obstacles and factors over which people have no control, SOAR aims to build or rebuild organizations around what works, rather than trying to fix what doesn't. Admittedly, I have never participated in a SOAR session, so I cannot discuss it based on personal involvement. I do encourage you to explore it further should this capture your interest.

Keyword search:

- Appreciative Inquiry Commons
- Center for Appreciative Inquiry

(I-4) SEEDPIT ANALYSIS

A common element of situation analyses is titled PEST or PESTEL. These acronyms represent the external political, economic, social, technological, and/or environmental and legal climates and trends affecting your business. I have developed a new acronym, SEEDPIT, that also encompasses demographics and industrial and professional trends.

The following chart includes some examples of each.

Social/Cultural: Popular culture trends, media influences, unemployment, and other social and cultural issues

Economic: Current economic climate, locally and nationally

Environmental: Trends related to the environment, weather patterns, the "green" movement, and ecological issues

Demographic: Current demographics (population age, geography, income level, gender) and shifting demographic trends

Political/Regulatory: Relevant governmental and legislative issues

Industrial/Professional: Changing trends and issues related to your industry or profession

Technological: Technological changes, recent innovations, new digital marketing channels

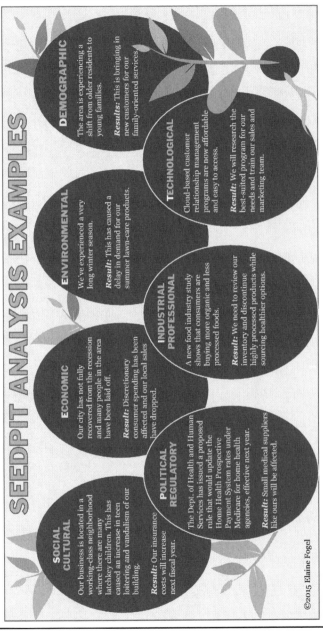

Develop a list for each relevant SEEDPIT trend currently affecting your small business.

SEEDPIT ANALYSIS EXAMPLES

SOCIAL CULTURAL

Our business is located in a working-class neighborhood where there are many latchkey children. This has caused an increase in teen loitering and vandalism of our building.

Result: Our insurance costs will increase next fiscal year.

POLITICAL REGULATORY

The Dept. of Health and Human Services has issued a proposed rule that would update the Home Health Prospective Payment System rates under Medicare for home health agencies, effective next year.

Result: Small medical suppliers like ours will be affected.

ECONOMIC

Our city has not fully recovered from the recession and many people in the area have been laid off.

Result: Discretionary consumer spending has been affected and our local sales have dropped.

INDUSTRIAL PROFESSIONAL

A new food industry study shows that consumers are buying more organic and less processed foods.

Result: We need to review our inventory and discontinue highly processed products while sourcing healthier options.

ENVIRONMENTAL

We've experienced a very long winter season.

Result: This has caused a delay in demand for our summer lawn-care products.

DEMOGRAPHIC

The area is experiencing a shift from older residents to young families.

Results: This is bringing in new customers for our family-oriented services

TECHNOLOGICAL

Cloud-based customer relationship management programs are now affordable and easy to access.

Result: We will research the best-suited program for our needs and train our sales and marketing team.

©2015 Elaine Fogel

For a better view, download the image (in color) from: http://elainefogel.com/seedpit.jpg

I-5) COMPETITIVE & COLLABORATIVE ANALYSIS

To the best of your ability, research your competition using accessible sources such as websites, blogs, and social media networks. Ask people you know if they have any experience with competitors' products or services. What feedback can you garner?

For B2C companies, visit competitors' locations, where feasible. For B2B companies, attend trade shows where competitors might be exhibiting. If your business depends on local customers, drive around your immediate area and look for competitors. Sign up for competitors' newsletters and e-mail subscriptions to check on their activities.

You'll want to do the following:

- Identify which products and/or services your business has in common with competitors. How does pricing compare with yours?

- List relevant differences in benefits and features of what your business offers compared with other providers. Which marketing strategies and tactics do they use and to what degree of success?

- Identify their strengths and weaknesses. Do they pose a threat or opportunity for your business?

Conducting a collaborative analysis is a newer practice and used primarily to identify and evaluate your company's existing partnerships, as well as assess internal opportunities for collaboration. I have used it in the nonprofit sector where resources are often tight and organizations can greatly benefit from joint cooperation.

- Identify your current business partners and how you collaborate. (If you have none, proceed to I-6, Market Analysis.) How do these partnerships help reduce your overhead or other expenses? How does your business benefit from the arrangement?

Examples:

- "We share space and/or resources with our box supplier, reducing our infrastructure costs by 27%."

- "We provide free packaging services for the company next door. Once we return their packaged products, they take care of their own shipping. In return, their bookkeeper manages our payroll."

I-6) MARKET SEGMENTATION & TARGET ANALYSIS

This section helps you analyze your customers and markets in more detail. Many small businesses that fail to conduct this exercise can easily spin their wheels trying to reach too broad an audience.

When you focus on your company's smaller market segments (audiences), you can target your ideal customers much easier. This yields a bigger bang for your marketing buck and makes marketing more manageable with limited resources. Once your revenue increases, you can add employees or outsourced individuals to help manage new segments or build on existing ones.

Look for secondary research available online to help you.

Secondary Research:

"Market research that's already compiled and organized for you. Examples of secondary information include reports and studies by government agencies, trade associations or other businesses within your industry."(Entrepreneur.com)

- For B2C companies, list any demographic and psychographic information you have or can find out about your company's target market segments/ audiences. Who are its ideal customers?

Demographics:

Statistical figures for a specific population related to race, age, income, education, religion, disabilities, home ownership, occupation, languages spoken, marital/ relationship status, family size, and employment status.

Psychographics:

Attitudes, preferences, beliefs, and lifestyles of a particular segment of a population.

- Identify which specific products and/or services each market segment buys. What are segment customers' primary motivations for purchasing these products and/or services? What are their emotional triggers? What do they value?

- Examine each segment's position in the sales cycle, too. Review each step from initial introduction through closing or sales transaction. Are there any noteworthy commonalities?

- Identify which marketing communications channels your target audiences prefer. For instance, do they get their information from traditional or digital sources? i.e. television, radio, newspapers, magazines, websites, e-newsletters, social media, or other places? If you don't know, you can conduct an online survey.

- Identify which referral sources are important to your business. These are the people who refer others to your company. Are they former or current customers, online reviewers, employees, suppliers, or others? Where can you reach them to create positive brand awareness and increase referrals for your company?

- For B2B companies, list any firmographic information you have or can find out.

Firmographics:

Information on business (or organization) customers that can include company size, type, location, years in business, number of employees, annual revenue, NAICS classification (North American Industry Classification System), and credit report.

You can also identify these customers by position in the sales cycle, purchasing behavior, company loyalty, sector (public, private), or any other appropriate way for your specific business. There's no right or wrong method here, but the more information you explore, the more insights you can gain.

- List the most common decision makers in each market segment. What are their titles, ages, educational level, etc.? What are their common goals, issues, work experiences, and attitudes? See if there are any similarities.

- Identify which specific products and/or services each market segment typically purchases. What are their primary motivations for buying? Which problems are your products and/or services solving? Which factors represent the best opportunities for continuing and future sales?

- Identify which marketing communication channels and content your business segments prefer. Do they typically get their business-related information from websites, newsletters, e-mails, videos, trade publications, mobile devices, the Internet, trade shows, social media, etc.? Ask a cross section of current customers to get a feel for their preferences.

- List the referral sources (groups or individuals) who refer your services/products to new customers. Where can you reach them to create positive brand awareness and increase referrals for your company?

- For both B2C and B2B companies, state your company's pricing structure. If you're unfamiliar with this part, check out this excellent video, "How to Determine Price in Each Marketing Structure in Terms of Maximizing Profit," by Jackie Jackson of Demand Media. (The link is in the Resources section.

- List your business' product/service distribution channels.

Distribution Channels:

"The chain of businesses or intermediaries through which a good or service passes until it reaches the end consumer. A distribution channel can include wholesalers, retailers, distributors and even the internet."
(Investopedia US, A Division of IAC)

Example: Manufacturer to distributor, distributor to retailer, retailer to customer

I-7) BRAND ANALYSIS

Brand Perceptions Analysis

It's important to understand your stakeholders' brand perceptions – what they think, believe, feel, and say about your brand. Do they see your products, services, or business as reliable, cheap, expensive, customer focused, trusted, etc.? Research a sampling of current customers, prospects, suppliers, management, and employees.

You can accomplish this task on your own if you have the time to make some phone calls. It will be less thorough and scientific, but it can certainly provide some valuable insights that you may not have uncovered previously.

Before you start, be aware that many brand perceptions are subconscious and will not always come to the surface in interviews or surveys. Additionally, we know that respondents will frequently give answers they believe you want to hear. Regardless, you have to start somewhere.

See the Appendix for recommended brand research questions for current customers and suppliers, managers and employees, and B2B prospects.

Once you have completed this Brand Perceptions Analysis, create two lists – one of the brand perceptions you like and want to keep, and another of the ones you want to lose. Once you get to Marketing & Branding Plan Part II, incorporate the elements of the first list into your Branding Strategy wherever appropriate, to ensure you are reinforcing the ones you want to keep.

Retain the second list, too. Once you get to Marketing & Branding Plan Part IV and establish customer surveys to evaluate your marketing and branding tactics, you can check your progress to see if these unwanted perceptions are waning. If not, adjust your strategy and/or tactics accordingly.

Brand Identity Audit

Take the time to audit your current business brand identity. Pull all your internal and external print marketing communications together and spread them out on a table. These include business cards, posters, brochures, catalogs, flyers, sales letters, promotional products, etc. If you're a solopreneur, ask a few good friends or family members to help you with the audit.

Go through each one and evaluate whether they look consistent and use the same logos, typography, colors, design elements, and style. Do you they have consistent messaging and tone?

Now review any outdoor collateral (signage, billboards, banners, etc.) and digital marketing communications (websites, blogs, social media pages, e-mails, newsletters, etc.) and evaluate them as well. How does your digital collateral appear in each communication channel, including different mobile devices?

Brand Reputation Analysis

The Internet provides the tools to check your small business' online brand reputation. One of the least costly ways to find out what others are saying about your company is by using Google Alerts.

You can set up alerts for a variety of names and keywords, such as your company name and any of its variations, the names of the business owner and employees who are posting company content, and product or service names. You can also check the feedback about your major competitors.

Google can send you daily or weekly alerts, or as they happen. I personally find them very effective. A free online reputation tool called IceRocket (by Meltwater) allows you to check blogs, Twitter, and Facebook.

I also recommend browsing business review sites such as Citysearch, Consumer Search, Google My Business, Insider Pages, Local.com, Sitejabber, Yahoo! Local, and Yelp! Most of these sites cater to consumers while Manta includes B2B company reviews.

Take the time to check the buzz for your business as part of this plan. Record any significant discoveries so you can include relevant metrics when you get to Marketing & Branding Plan Part IV.

II. MARKETING & BRANDING STRATEGY

Your small business' marketing and branding strategy will determine many factors, one of which is to identify the source of the biggest bang for the dollar. It will also give your company a roadmap for daily marketing and branding activities so you don't end up wasting time, energy, and money on unproductive tactics.

Your strategy begins with identifying your company's marketing and branding objectives. Review your plan up to this point and determine the objectives you want to tackle.

(II-1) MARKETING & BRANDING OBJECTIVES

Aside from reaching your revenue goals, state your general marketing and branding objectives as they relate to your company's products and/or services, pricing, distribution channels, and marketing communications.

Objectives should always be SMART, an acronym with which you may be familiar. It was originally defined by George Doran, Arthur Miller, and James Cunningham in a 1981 issue of Management Review. (*Wikipedia*, SMART criteria)

Although there are variations on the SMART theme, I have selected the following for our purposes:

Specific: Be specific with your goals.

Measurable: Ensure you can quantify and measure your objectives.

Assignable: State who is responsible for meeting each objective.

Realistic: Set achievable targets for your company, taking its financial and human resources into account.

Time-Based: Set timeframes for attaining each objective.

Examples:

- Increase customer loyalty for [product name] by retaining 15% more of its customers this year. Responsibility: David H. and me

- Launch [new service] as a complement to [existing one] by next summer, using our Q2 net profits and tax rebate. Responsibility: Janet W., Dannell R., and me

(II-2) KEYS TO SUCCESS

List the factors that will contribute to achieving each marketing and branding objective. What will it take to succeed?

Examples:

- To succeed at increasing sales by 22%, we need to hire two additional salespeople.

- To succeed at improving brand awareness for our company and increasing leads by 10%, we will develop and test a three-month, multichannel marketing campaign.

(II-3) BRAND POSITIONING STRATEGY

Brand Positioning Strategy:

The way you frame your brand/products and/or services to each market segment. It's also how your segments perceive them.

Positioning your brand represents short-term communication objectives... It should be based on those parts of the brand vision that will resonate with the market, support the current business strategy, and reflect the current reality of what the brand can credibly deliver. (David Aaker, *Aaker on Branding: 20 Principles That Drive Success*)

Positioning typically focuses on how buyers use your products and/or services, their relevance to customers' lives or companies' needs, how different, unique, or beneficial they are, which audiences use them, their quality, how they solve problems, how they save money, or how they stack up to competitors. Alternatively, you may decide to concentrate on the emotional side of your brand.

Do your company values set your brand/products and/or services apart? Do your products and/or services help customers impress others, enhance their appearance, boost their self-esteem, help them feel important, or make them look good to their bosses?

If your products and/or services are specific to one market segment or industry (B2B), plan how you will position them for each. Will you position them based on pricing, easy availability, exclusivity to specific locations or channels, or other factors?

Examples:

No-frills airlines such as Jet Blue, Southwest, and WestJet employ similar positioning strategies. They offer customers a quality flying experience for lower fares, without the frills that competitors provide. They focus on enjoyment and the customer experience to gain brand loyalty. Southwest Airlines takes its competitive advantage even further by being the only airline that doesn't charge passengers for checking one or two bags.

If you want to watch an amazing brand in action, check this WestJet video. It demonstrates the airline's philanthropic angle. http://youtu.be/zIEIvi2MuEk

Build your own positioning strategies for each segment to help develop your company's marketing messages.

(II-4) KEY MESSAGES

Key Messages:

The main points you want your target market segments to remember about your business, products, or services.

You can develop five to seven key messages for the overall business or for each of your company's positioning strategies, if they differ. Key messages should be concise, believable, positive, comprehensive, and strategic. You can draw on them for use in marketing collateral, news releases, content marketing, interviews, meetings, and sales presentations.

Examples:

- Test results show that our product will reduce your company's waste by 32%.

- Our team has 102 collective years of experience in this industry.

- Ten percent of every product sale goes to [charity name].

(II-5) MARKETING STRATEGIES

Marketing strategies identify the necessary steps to attain your business' overall objectives. These are higher-level ideas that typically take longer to achieve.

Examples:

- Drive traffic from social media sites to website landing pages.

- Promote and launch a new customer loyalty program.

- Develop a contest to acquire new customers.

- Once you have developed your small business' marketing strategies, it's time to work on the tactics that match each strategy.

(II-6) BRANDING STRATEGY

Brand Vision Statement

A brand vision statement is as important to your company's success as its mission, vision and values. It serves as a compass for employees and business owners.

Brand Vision Statement:

"An articulated description of the aspirational image for the brand; what you want the brand to stand for in the eyes of customers and other relevant groups like employees and partners." (David Aaker, *Aaker on Branding: 20 Principles That Drive Success*)

Examples:

- Amazon: "To be the world's most customer-centric company; to build a place where people can come to find and discover anything they might want to buy online."

- The Walt Disney Corporation: "To make people happy."

- Google: "To provide access to the world's information in one click."

- Here's one I developed for a generic health company: "To help our customers be the healthiest they can be." It's short and simple.

  If I add details: "To help our customers be the healthiest they can be through a focus on proper nutrition, exercise, wellness, and a positive attitude."

Get your employees together to brainstorm and come up with your company's brand vision statement.

Brand Values

 **Brand Values:**

The beliefs, actions, and behaviors your company delivers to, and shares with, its customers.

Examples:

- Helpful, reliable, accessible, caring, knowledgeable, innovative

Develop a list of your business' current brand values using the first list you created after performing the Brand Perceptions Analysis. Now add the values you believe your business currently has that were not mentioned previously.

Next, include the aspirational brand values you strive to impart to customers. These combined values will serve as metrics indicators when you get to Marketing & Branding Plan Part IV.

Brand Personality

Brand Personality:

When you give your brand human characteristics and personality. (See the Appendix, Brand Perceptions Analysis Research Questions, question #3)

Examples:

• Fun-loving, smart, helpful, trustworthy

Take the first list you created during the Brand Perceptions Analysis and include any item that refers to your company's brand personality. Now add any aspirational personality traits you'd like your business to impart.

Create a combined list of your company's brand personality here. As you continue this plan and after you complete it, ensure that your company's brand values, brand tone of voice, brand identity, and key messages are aligned with its preferred brand personality.

Example:

During the Brand Perceptions Analysis, you discover that one of the company's strongest brand personality traits is being very informative. Customers claim that they learn a lot from you and your team during interactions.

While that's a good thing, you'd also like them to notice your business' ability to inform in an entertaining way. By adding this aspirational brand personality trait to the list, you can incorporate the entertaining aspect into the company's informational marketing communications content, brand values, brand tone of voice, and key messages. This helps ensure brand consistency.

Brand Tone of Voice

Your business' brand tone of voice should realistically reflect its brand personality in all its marketing communications.

Example:

Suppose you import and sell children's educational toys.

One of the company's brand personality traits is likely going to be FUN.

Because the company markets to both parents and children, you'll want its marketing communications to appeal to both audiences independently. Parents want their kids to have fun while they're playing with toy products so they don't notice that they're learning something, too. Kids won't play with the toys unless they can have fun with them.

That means segregating your company's brand tone of voice into two segments – one for parents and one for their kids. The tone, mood, and content you use for kids will be simple, kid-centered, engaging, and focused on the fun they'll have playing with your toy products. The tone, mood, and content you use for parents will be adult-centered and informative, emphasizing what their children will learn as they play and have fun.

Brand Identity

Brand Identity:

Is how your customers perceive your brand, company, product, or service. However, in many marketing circles, it has come to represent the brand's visual elements such as colors, typography (font styles), symbols, graphics, marks, and logo.

The identity should reflect your company's brand personality and values, elicit trust, impart professionalism, and create a connection between the business and its target audiences.

If your company's current brand identity does not accomplish this purpose and the company is relatively new in the market, you can decide to re-brand the identity, ideally with assistance from marketing professionals. If your company has been around for a while and its brand identity has already been established, you may decide to keep or tweak it subtly.

There is another option for older companies. If you want to put new life into the business brand for any reason, you can refresh its brand identity. The company name can stay the same while you design a new logo, brand colors, etc. to better reflect an updated brand personality.

Whichever you decide, this is the place in the plan where you list the company's brand identity. Import the logo; state the colors, the preferred typography, and other brand identity components. (You may want to review the Bonus Material: Logo and Printing Tips first before completing this section.)

If your small business has many employees or several sub brands with different logos, you should consider developing guidelines for brand identity standards that include:

- Logo guides and usage
- Color schemes
- Typography styles
- Web standards
- Trademark standards
- Spelling standards

Visit a couple of university websites and search for their brand identity guidelines. Their templates can help guide you through the process.

Brand Promise

Brand Promise:

Represents what a brand promises to deliver to stakeholders and customers – focused on the benefits for them.

Although the brand promise is a synopsis of what your company does and for whom, most stakeholders won't be aware of its exact words. But that's not atypical; it is more of an internal document.

What you do want is for them to be aware of their positive feelings and experiences as a result of your brand promise. You want them to rave about the brand, trust in it, and remain loyal to it.

But this doesn't happen by osmosis. By placing the brand promise at the center of everything you and any employees do, you'll be focused on delivering it consistently. After all, it wouldn't be worth much if it only represented a promise without the business actually delivering on it.

Once you have developed your company's brand vision statement and brand values, you can begin to work on its brand promise. Don't be surprised if the promise is similar to the company's mission statement. They both represent the business' purpose for existence.

Here's a corporate example that demonstrates the differences among the mission statement, vision statement, and brand promise. It comes from Tim Hortons®, one of the largest, publicly traded, quick service restaurant chains in North America (based on market capitalization) and the largest in Canada.

The restaurant is famous for its legendary coffee (brewed fresh every 20 minutes), as well as donuts and other menu items. Just ask Canucks (Canadians) about it and you'll likely see a big grin of pride on their faces.

- Mission statement: "To deliver superior quality products and services for our guests and communities through leadership, innovation and partnerships."

- Vision statement: "To be the quality leader in everything we do."

- Brand promise: "Prepared fresh to order, with the same great quality and taste, at an affordable price, every time."

To give you more brand promise ideas:

- NFL: "To be the premier sports and entertainment brand that brings people together, connecting them socially and emotionally like no other."

- Hilton: "To ensure every Guest feels cared for, valued and respected and we continue Conrad Hilton's mission to fill the earth with the light and warmth of hospitality."

- Target: "Expect More. Pay Less."

III. MARKETING & BRANDING TACTICS

Tactics:

The shorter-term actionable tasks performed as a result of defining strategies.

Multitudes of marketing tactics are available, so it's important to review what you have written so far in this plan. Ensure that the tactics match your strategies, which in turn, fulfill the company's objectives. Choose tactics that are affordable, manageable (for you or whoever is responsible), and will engage your target market segments in the channels where they "hang out."

Examples:

- Exhibit at XYZ trade show to access prospective clients.

- Create targeted Facebook ads to attract more prospects and customers.

- Sponsor a table at [charity name] fundraising dinner to demonstrate commitment to [name of business partner being honored].

Many of your small business' marketing and branding tactics will encompass marketing communications, so let's begin here.

(III-1) MARKETING COMMUNICATIONS

Marketing Communications:

The customary promotional (and now nonpromotional) components of marketing. These are the messages your business develops and uses to communicate in traditional (such as radio) and digital (such as social media) channels.

Years ago, marketing communications were more about "pushing" promotional messages out to target audiences. Now these include engaging with prospects and customers and building networks of followers, fans, and friends.

Content Marketing

Content marketing has become one of the most popular methods of reaching new audiences and engaging current ones.

Content Marketing:

"A marketing technique of creating and distributing valuable, relevant and consistent content to attract and acquire a clearly defined audience – with the objective of driving profitable customer action." (Content Marketing Institute)

Content includes the nonpromotional information your company shares externally, such as blog posts, white papers, newsletters, slide shows, or research data. It establishes your business as a leader in its areas of expertise and works to attract its target market segments.

But as widespread as content marketing is, putting all your marketing eggs into one basket would be foolhardy.

Recent studies have shown how different audiences prefer certain channels over others. Results can be quite surprising and go against typical assumptions.

Example: Millennials (born between 1981 and 1995) may
not always prefer digital channels over traditional ones. (That's why it is so important to keep abreast of current marketing trends.)

Integrated Marketing Communications

In addition to self-publishing content online, marketing communications also include many other activities and channel choices.

Integrated Marketing Communications:

The process of using consistent messages that reinforce one another in the appropriate channels or media used.

Multichannel Marketing:

The process of using a variety of marketing channels that fit with your target audiences, to communicate and engage with them.

Example:
If you're running a customer acquisition campaign, your messages should be consistent in the e-mails you send, the social media messages you post, and the postcards you mail. That means using the same images and copy with slight variations to accommodate each specific channel's requirements.

The following list of marketing communication channels is extensive, so don't feel overwhelmed by it. As a small business owner or professional, select the most ideal channels to target your prospects and customers that can produce the highest return on your marketing dollar (ROMD). This means that you'll want to choose those that deliver your marketing messages and engage the most people in your audiences at the lowest possible cost.

Be strategic. Start with less and test your tactics before adding new channels.

Marketing Communications Channels

- Affiliate marketing
- Audio podcasting
- Benches
- Billboards
- Blogs
- Brochures
- Business cards
- Catalogs
- Cause marketing
- Conferences
- Content
- Contests
- Coupons and discounting
- Direct mail (addressed or Every Door Direct Mail®)
- Direct response
- Directory listings
- Doorhangers
- Elevators
- E-mails

- Flyers
- Google AdSense
- In store
- In-stream video ads
- Kiosks
- Landing pages
- Magazines (print and electronic)
- Movie screens
- Newsletters (print and electronic)
- Newspapers (print and electronic)
- Networking
- Online display ads
- Pay-per-click (cost per lead, cost per impression, cost per action)
- Personal selling
- Point of purchase
- Posters and signs
- Presentations
- Promotional products
- Public relations
- Public speaking
- Radio
- Search engines
- Seminars
- Social media ads (Twitter, Facebook, LinkedIn)
- Social media networking

- Special events
- Sponsorships
- Telemarketing
- Television
- Texting
- Trade shows
- Transit (shelters, subways, buses, and trains)
- Videos
- Websites
- Word of mouth

(III-2) MARKETING MIX

Marketing Mix:

An older term that refers to the 4 Ps of marketing: product, price, place, and promotion.

Product:

What your business sells to its target audiences (includes name, brand identity, appearance, packaging, functions, features, benefits).

Price:

How you price your goods and services (value, discounts, seasonal, sale pricing).

Place:

Where you sell your company's goods and services (distribution, locations, inventory, shipping).

Promotion:

How you promote your goods and services to target market segments (advertising, sales, public relations, marketing communications).

Because marketing is no longer about "pushing" messages out to buyers by interrupting them to hear you, marketers can now directly engage with their target audiences, drawing them in through the different stages of the new sales cycle. First, prospective customers become aware of your business' brand or its products and services. This may be the result of content marketing, word-of-mouth referrals, search engines, webinars, and other channels that attract their interest.

After prospective customers see the same messages in multiple channels, they may be more keenly interested in your business' products or services. If they decide to explore more about your business, they can research review sites, browse your website, or ask others if they have heard of your company. They can also contact your business to seek further information. That's the perfect time for you (or sales people) to engage with prospects further, solving their problems and fulfilling their needs. If prospects are not interested at that moment, they may (or may not) bookmark your site or file your company information for future reference.

After prospective customers have completed their research, they then make a decision whether or not to make a purchase. If they do, they convert into customers and the relationship continues.

You want to thank these new customers, engage them, and give them reasons to stay loyal to your business. The ultimate goal is to earn their trust so they become one of your company's brand ambassadors, tooting your horn for you.

As you begin to tackle this marketing mix exercise, let's simplify things. Let's work with a marketing mix based on the 5 Ws of journalism.

- **WHO**: To whom are you marketing? Identify your target audiences.

- **WHAT**: What products or services are you promoting to each audience?

- **WHERE**: Where are you marketing to each audience? Where are your products and services available? Which marketing communication channels are you using to reach out to each target audience?

- **WHEN**: When are you marketing to each audience? What is the time frame for each tactic?

- **WHY**: Why are you marketing to each audience? What is the associated strategy?

On the next page, you'll see a matrix of this model with an example for a B2C cosmetics company. Please note that this represents the beginning of writing the mix and is by no means a complete matrix.

For a better view, download the matrix (in color) from:
http://elainefogel.com/cosmetics-b2c-example.jpg

COSMETICS COMPANY B2C EXAMPLE

WHO	WHAT	WHERE	WHEN	WHY
North American urban women, 35-55, with college education and combined family income of $75K+	High-end anti-aging skin care product line	Select in-store demos, distribute samples, collect entries for draw to win full product line gift set	4 weeks leading up to Mother's Day	•Brand awareness •Put product into prospects' hands to try •Build-word-of-mouth buzz
		Ongoing email marketing campaign: thank-you follow up, link to time-bound discount code for online ordering; newsletters with articles on skincare written by dermatologist	Beginning within 2 days of each prospect completing a draw entry	•Continued brand awareness •Discount incentive to longer-term product trial •Begin to build relationship
		Online media releases via wire service announcing prize winners	Monday following Mother's Day	•Brand awareness

©Elaine Fogel 2015

If you find that your marketing mix is heavier in one channel than in another, you may decide to drill down even further.

Example:

If you rely a lot on content or social media marketing, you can develop a separate, auxiliary plan for these channels. Of course, this will depend on having the time availability, inclination, and desire to go into more detail. However, it will be a valuable asset for evaluation purposes.

(III-3) ACTION PLAN

Once you complete the final marketing mix, you can add details to create your action plan. The action plan will guide you through the steps required to complete each marketing and/or branding tactic and should also include the following:

- An estimated budget for each tactic.

- Who is responsible for implementation and/or oversight.

- Materials or equipment required.

- Deadline for each task. Work backwards from the date of the completed tactic to establish a reasonable timeline of activities. (Always allow more time to accommodate any setbacks or delays.)

Once you add estimated budgets and timelines for each tactic in the marketing mix, you may discover that you cannot possibly do them all. This is the time to identify your priorities while you put others on hold until you have the necessary resources.

You can create an action plan for each month, each quarter, or an entire year. I wouldn't advise going further because things change so quickly that you'll find yourself re-doing it if you plan too far in advance. As it is, you'll be tweaking the plan as you go along, making adjustments as you measure results.

No matter how organized you believe you and your team are, developing a structured action plan will keep everyone on track and accountable to one another. If you have project management software that can make things easier, by all means, use it. If not, Microsoft Excel® spreadsheets can work, too.

In keeping with the marketing mix matrix sample I provided, I have added the beginning of an action plan. Feel free to adjust the template in any way that works for you. My example is not set in stone.

For a better view, download the matrix (in color) from:
http://elainefogel.com/cosmetics-b2c-action-plan.jpg

COSMETICS COMPANY B2C ACTION PLAN EXAMPLE

IN-STORE DEMOS OF PRODUCT LINE

DEADLINE	TACTIC	ACTION	BUDGET	RESPONSIBILITY	✓
February 13	Recruit 10-12 local cosmetics and department store customers to host in-store demos	Contact store managers or buyers and discuss program	N/A	Latonya Jones	
March 2	Develop training program for event and merchandising specialists	Using existing marketing collateral and team input, develop half-day training program and booklet	N/A	George Mills	
March 2	Recruit 25 event and merchandising specialists	Call XYZ Product Demonstration Group to book event and merchandising specialists	$20,000	Latonya Jones	
March 6	Review and revise training program	Distribute training materials and elicit feedback from team, make necessary revisions.	N/A	George Mills	
March 9	Design training materials	Give marketing agency the copy and creative brief to design the training materials.	$1200	George Mills	
March 20	Review, revise, and approve materials design.	Sign off on training materials.	N/A	George Mills	
March 23	Print 50 copies of training materials. 8½" x 11", 32-page saddle stitch, 4/4	Send PDF files to print broker.	$500	George Mills	
April 1	Training program	Train event and merchandising specialists on product line and responsibilities	$2000	Julia Rodriguez	

©Elaine Fogel 2015

IV. METRICS

This part of the marketing plan is essential in determining what's working and what's not. Review the tactics in your action plan and determine the key performance indicators for each one.

 **Key Performance Indicators (KPIs):**
The desired outcomes or indicators of any objective that defines and measures what success will look like if achieved.

Example: Let's say one of your marketing objectives is to increase the number of company newsletter subscribers by 20% this fiscal year in order to reach more prospective customers. The associated marketing strategy is to promote the benefits of newsletter subscription.

For marketing tactics, you plan to add a pop-up form and widget on the company blog, listing some benefits; include a subscription form on every web page; and include a link to the subscription page in every employee e-mail signature. The subscription landing page will detail the newsletter's benefits and include a sample.

The KPI would be to achieve a 20% lift in subscriptions from each tactic or overall. Because measurement is an ongoing process, you'll be able to evaluate which tactics are performing better than others and which might be bombing. Then you can make the necessary adjustments to increase your chances of success. Why spin your wheels if you're not getting anywhere, right?

Here are a few more KPI examples:

- Increased inbound website visitors by 10%.
- Increased e-mail subscriber opt-ins by 12%.

- Improved lead-to-conversion rate by 9%.
- Increased number of referrals by 20%.
- Increased positive customer reviews by 25%.
- Improved direct mail response rates by 1%.

(IV-1) WHAT TO MEASURE

You can use many methods to measure your company's KPIs. Depending on its strategies and tactics, as well as the selected marketing communication channels, existing tools can make this task less tedious.

According to eMarketer's *The State of Digital Display 2014: An Industry Readying Itself for Brand Advertisers*:

US spending on digital display ads will grow faster than any other format as companies in the digital display advertising ecosystem seek to further prove display a compelling storytelling medium for brands. (This type of advertising includes banner ads, video, Flash rich media, HTML5 Rich Media, and sponsorships.)

At the time of writing this book, digital display advertising is in a state of change. Even though many marketers will still measure engagement by clicks, click-through rates (CTR), impressions, and interactions, the industry is moving towards *viewable impressions* as a standard.

The rationale for the change is that impressions cannot determine whether visitors actually saw or engaged with ads or not. Digital display ads that appear too low on web pages, or videos that run on small default video players, can show up as impressions even though visitors didn't actually view them.

Worse yet, impressions count when robots visit websites. According to a 2013 study by Incapsula, these robot visits can account for 61% of all web traffic.

To solve the problem, the American Association of Advertising Agencies, Association of National Advertisers, and Interactive Advertising Bureau have collaborated on "Making Measurement Make Sense" (3MS) to "define and drive clear standards-based metrics for interactive advertising, across the marketing ecosystem, that are comparable to legacy media."

So if your small business runs digital display advertising campaigns, I recommend that you visit the 3MS site to learn more about these new standards and how to measure them. I suspect that these metrics will evolve with technological advances.

Website and Blog Metrics

Google Analytics, which offers free and upgraded formats, is an excellent measurement tool for most small businesses. It measures visitor demographics and behaviors, page views, active pages, social traffic, keywords, referral pages, visitor languages and locations, conversion rates, and a lot more.

What you require will depend on how sophisticated your company's needs are. If you need assistance understanding how the program works, Google offers an Analytics Help Center with video tutorials.

Other web measurement options include Alexa, Crazy Egg, Open Site Explorer by Moz, SeeVolution, and StatsCrop.

E-Mail Marketing Metrics

E-mail marketing is relatively easy to track and measure. Your e-mail service provider (ESP) should have all the data you need to evaluate your company's efforts. Depending on your e-mail marketing KPIs, here's a list of some things to measure (except open rate):

- New subscribers. These reflect how many new people sign up to receive your e-mails.

- Click-throughs. These show how many people click on links in your e-mails. Look for unique clicks that measure the number of individuals, disregarding how many times each one may have clicked.

- Conversions. These indicate how many people follow your calls to action (CTA). For example, if you include a link in your e-mail to download a white paper, then the number of people who download it, compared to the number of e-mails you send, gives you the conversion rate.

- Bounces. These reveal the number of e-mails that don't reach intended recipients. This situation can result from temporary issues with recipients' servers or permanent problems like recipients' e-mail addresses that are no longer valid.

Here's a good tip from Sarah Goliger at HubSpot:

You should immediately remove hard [permanent] bounce addresses from your e-mail list, because internet service providers (ISPs) use bounce rates as one of the key factors to determine an email sender's reputation. Having too many hard bounces can make your company look like a spammer in the eyes of an ISP. (2014)

- Forwards. These reflect how many times recipients forward your e-mails to others.

- Unsubscribes. These indicate how many recipients cancel their subscriptions to your e-mails.

- Open rate. This shows the number of people who open your e-mails. ESPs track this data by measuring embedded graphic image downloads. The downside to this metric is that it isn't always accurate. There are some conditions where ESPs cannot track open rates:

Text e-mails have no graphic images to track. Some desktop, mobile, and web-based e-mail software programs automatically block image downloads by default. The only way to overcome this issue is to ask recipients to add your e-mail address to their address books. Realistically, you'll never get 100% compliance on this; hence the open rate isn't a valid metric.

Social Media Metrics

Many available tools can measure your business' social media (SM) marketing efforts. Which tools you use will depend on the nature of your small business and the number of its SM marketing accounts.

For sole proprietorships or businesses that have few employees participating in social networking, there are many free and low-cost SM monitoring and management sites. These include: Buffer, Crowdbooster, Hootsuite, Likeable Local, and Social Report. You can also check out SimplyMeasured for its free social media analytics tools. For companies with many SM accounts, profiles, and users, the suppliers above offer upgraded pricing options to accommodate your needs.

What to track

Many people believe that tracking the increases in followers, fans, and "likes" provides valuable data. But as Tom Cruise's character says in the film *Jerry Maguire*, "Show me the money!"

It doesn't really matter how many people follow you on SM. What matters is how many of them fall within your target audiences, respond to your CTA or content, and become sharers, business leads, and customers.

After all, SM marketing is but one marketing mix component to reach and engage with prospective and existing customers. If you don't use it strategically, you'll be wasting a lot of time online without much to show for it.

That's not to say that you shouldn't celebrate increasing your SM reach. The more people who read your messages, share them, and engage with you, the better chances that new people will see your brand and perhaps take action to connect. I'm just cautioning you that when it comes to SM, quality connections often beat quantity.

Although there are many ways to measure SM marketing, I'm including those that I believe are most relevant to small businesses:

- *Engagement and influence.* This reflects how people interact and respond to your SM messages. You want to gauge how many replies, comments, "likes," mentions, clicks, shares, Google +1s, and responses you receive. The greater the engagement activity at the "right" time with the "right" people, the more brand exposure, search engine results, inbound leads, reach, influence, web traffic, conversions, and sales you can attain.

- **Conversions.** These indicate how many times your SM "friends" take action. If they make a purchase, download a white paper or e-book, or sign up for your company newsletter, these are considered conversions.

- **Traffic generation.** This shows the number of visits you get on your website, blog, and/or landing pages that come from SM channels. Google Analytics can provide this data.

- **Net promoter score.** This identifies your company's customers under three categories: promoters, passives, and detractors. Net Promoter (http://www.netpromoter.com) is a powerful management philosophy: both a loyalty metric and a discipline for using customer feedback to fuel profitable growth in your business.

- **Timing.** This reveals the best times and days of the week to post and engage. As you evaluate your SM participation, check to see which times and days receive the most engagement so you know when to share important content.

- **Revenue.** Ultimately, most small businesses practice SM marketing to increase their revenue. Tracking revenue growth will depend on your company's strategy and selected SM tools.

Customer and Employee Insights

Understanding your customers and employees is crucial to your small business' success. You want to retain them as your company's best brand ambassadors, but only if you can keep them happy and empowered. The best way to know where you stand is to simply ask them. Some of the customer insights you may want to uncover are:

- What they believe about your brand, marketing messages, products, or services.

- Their needs and desires.

- How they rate your company's customer service.

- What their buying habits are and motivators in purchasing your products or services.

- How satisfied they are with your products and services.

- What they're willing to pay for your products and services and why.

- Whether they would recommend your products and services and why.

Some of the employee insights you may want to uncover are:

- Their levels of job satisfaction.

- Whether they feel empowered, recognized, and appreciated at work.

- Their motivation levels.

- Their evaluation of management.

- Whether they feel that their talents and skills are being utilized at work.

- Their ability to balance work and life in their jobs.

- Whether they have a clear understanding of the company's objectives, mission, and vision.

- Whether they receive constructive feedback from their supervisors.

- Whether they feel part of a team.

- Whether they believe that the company addresses its customers' needs.

- Whether they believe they are fairly compensated.

The list can continue, depending on how much you want to measure. Remember that employees can also provide valuable information and insight on your company's customers.

If your business has the funds to hire a reputable marketing research firm to conduct customer and employee research for you, I'd recommend you do that. If not, you do have some self-serve options.

First, you'll need to know which marketing research methods to use. Although newer neuro-scientific and technological methods are now available, they are costly. Therefore, I'd recommend using the traditional methods of qualitative and quantitative marketing research.

Qualitative Marketing Research

 **Qualitative Marketing Research:**
A research method that helps uncover respondents' feelings, behaviors, attitudes, perspectives, and needs.

You can conduct qualitative marketing research with small groups or individuals who represent your customers or employees using focus groups and in-depth interviews. Focus groups include five to eight participants in a moderated discussion. An in-depth interview (IDI) is a one-on-one interview either on the telephone or in person. This method enables participants to talk freely without others present.

If you had the money to pay a professional researcher for only one type of research, then qualitative research would be your best bet. If you were to conduct your own focus groups or IDIs, chances are that participants will self-monitor what they say and you won't get as accurate a picture as when an impartial outsider does the work.

The second choice would be to hire a university marketing student, preferably one who specializes in research and is at the post-graduate level. If neither option is feasible, you can create your own guidelines and invite a sampling of customers or employees to participate.

It's important to assure participants that they are free to say anything in total confidence without repercussion (and mean it, especially for employees). Ideally, audiotape the discussion so you can record exact quotes and valuable perceptions for later use and analysis.

Conduct your focus groups offsite, if possible, to allow for freer discussion away from the work environment. It's also customary to serve participants a meal or snacks.

Quantitative Marketing Research

Quantitative Marketing Research:

A research method that uses surveys and statistics to test a hypothesis (assumption) or specific question. Survey questions are close ended and participants must choose the best or most appropriate responses from a list of possible answers or rating scales.

This type of research would enable you to include all your business' customers or employees, as it is better suited for larger numbers of participants. Many free and low-cost customer survey sites can help you conduct quantitative research.

Some include: Instant.ly, LimeSurvey® (a free open-source survey application), ProProfs, QuestionPro, SoGoSurvey, SurveyGizmo, SurveyMonkey, SurveyMonster, SurveyTool, and Toluna QuickSurveys.

A couple of important points to know: Developing unbiased and effective surveys is an art and a science. It's easy for amateurs to skew results by asking questions incorrectly. Effective survey design resources come from HubSpot and Infusionsoft. *The Art of Asking Survey Questions* and *Customer Surveys: How to Raise Your Sales & Marketing IQ in 6 Easy Steps* are free downloadable e-books.

Revenue-Based Metrics

Revenue-Based Metrics:

Measures the tactics that lead to sales and revenue generation.

Track how many inbound inquiries you receive for your business' products and/or services. This happens when prospects call, e-mail, or complete web contact forms, as examples.

Measure how many leads your sales team has nurtured and are ready to make a purchase or sign a contract. Measurement can also include the number of hot prospects who have truly shown an interest in your company (several times in any given period) by downloading your content, commenting on your blog, sharing your SM posts, etc.

Other revenue-based metrics include measuring KPIs, referrals, opportunities, wins (sales), sales volume, sales revenue, cost per lead (CPL), cost to acquire customers, lifetime value of a customer, etc. Select the best revenue-based metric criteria that match your business needs.

IDEA #7 TAKEAWAY

You now have the tools and format to complete your small business' Marketing & Branding Plan. As demonstrated by the length of Idea #7's content, I can only reiterate the importance of developing a solid strategy. Sure, it can be a tedious project, but as I mentioned earlier, pick and choose which parts best suit your business and "just do it."

The key takeaway is: Write a plan, implement it, and measure it!

WRITE a plan.

IMPLEMENT it.

MEASURE it.

CONCLUSION

At this point, you can probably understand why I called this book *Beyond Your Logo*. Your small business' brand encompasses many components beyond its symbols, colors, logo, and appearances. It extends to the mindsets, attitudes, and behaviors of everyone involved in it. Your collective words, actions, interactions, stories, appearances, beliefs, practices, and approaches – both internally and externally – have a profound impact on your company's ability to deliver on its promises, gain a solid and positive reputation, and succeed.

Hopefully, you've gained some new insights and can take away a few tidbits that you can practically apply.

Thank you very much for reading the book. If you found it valuable, please add your review on one of the websites where it's available for purchase and tell your social network!

Feel free to send me an e-mail with your feedback, too. I'd love to hear from you.

Here's to your small business' success!

Elaine

Elaine Fogel
elaine@BeyondYourLogo.com

APPENDIX

BRAND PERCEPTIONS ANALYSIS RESEARCH QUESTIONS

CURRENT CUSTOMERS AND SUPPLIERS

Here's a list of some sample questions you can ask current customers and suppliers in person or on the telephone. Adjust them for B2C and B2B audiences.

1. How did you first hear about our company, products, or services?

2. Can you choose five to ten adjectives that describe the company/product/service/brand? (Ask for clarification or ask why they chose the words they did. This can reveal a lot.)

3. If this brand were a person, what personality traits would he or she have?

OR

4. If this brand were an animal/car/city, which would it be and why? (Choose whichever is more appropriate or use one of your own.)

5. Why did you choose our company/products/services? Did we meet your expectations? (For customers, not suppliers.)

6. Would you recommend this company/product/service/brand to others?

   (If yes) To whom? What would you tell them?
   (If no) Why not?

7. How could we improve our products and/or services to meet your needs better? (For customers, not suppliers.)

8. How would you rate our marketing communications, such as e-mails, newsletters, brochures, ads, blog, content, social media pages? (Choose those that are applicable and ask for individual ratings.)

   Excellent Very Good Good Fair Poor
   (Ask them to explain why they selected their answers.)

   Always send an appropriate thank-you note and/or a token gift afterwards to those who participated. For customers, offer a substantial discount, incentive, or free shipping on their next purchase.

MANAGERS AND EMPLOYEES

Here are some sample questions you can ask your company's managers and employees (if you have them):

1. In your opinion, what does our company do well internally and where can we improve? (Salary, working conditions, company policies, employee appreciation, etc.)

2. What do customers and suppliers tell you about the company? What have you heard from them about the quality and value of our products and services, our company's reputation, and our level of customer service?

3. What do you think our company's brand stands for?

B2B PROSPECTS

Interviewing B2B prospects can present a challenge. Instead of contacting complete strangers, ask current customers, colleagues, and friends for referrals. That way you can introduce yourself and mention their names.

Alternatively, contact people you know through networking, association membership, or from previous sales contacts. Make sure you state upfront that you're not calling to sell them anything. Briefly state exactly why you're calling, what you hope to achieve, and how much you'd appreciate a few minutes of their time to help you.

Always send an appropriate thank-you note and/or a token gift afterwards to those who participated. If you can, offer a substantial discount, incentive, or free shipping for a future purchase.

Depending on who you interview, here are some sample questions you can ask prospective customers. You may follow the suggested sequence or use your judgment and make any necessary adjustments as they respond.

1. Have you heard of our brand/company/products/ services previously?

   (If yes) From where? What did you initially hear about our brand/company/products/services? (This tells you which channels appear to be working and what people are saying.)

   (If no, skip questions 2–7 and proceed to the alternative list that follows.)

2. How would you rate our marketing communications, such as emails, newsletters, brochures, ads, blog, content, social media pages? (Choose those that are applicable and ask for individual ratings.)

   Excellent   Very Good   Good   Fair   Poor
   (Ask them to explain why they selected their answers.)

3. Have you ever made a purchase from us in the past?

   (If yes) What did you buy and why?
   (If no, proceed to question 7.)

4. Did it meet your expectations?

   (If yes) In what ways did it do so?
   (If no) How could we improve our products and/or services to meet your needs better?

5. Can you choose five to ten adjectives that describe the company/product/service/brand? (Ask for clarification or ask why they chose the words they did.)

6. Would you recommend this brand?

    (If yes) To whom? What would you tell them?
    (If no) Why not?

7. Do you typically purchase [state your products and/
    or services]?

    (If yes) Would you be interested in an introduction,
    meeting, or discount coupon? [or offer whatever
    suits your business.]
    (If no) Thank you for your time.

At the end of the call (whether these B2B prospects answer
yes or no to this last question), consider asking them to
refer other businesses that use your types of products and
services.

Alternative list of questions (if the answer to question 1
is "no")

1. What do you think our company name/brand
    means? Based on our name/brand, can you guess
    our business' products and services? (This tells you
    if the company name/brand can stand on its own or
    whether it needs a tagline or slogan to identify what
    the company does.)

2. (Now tell them what your business does or sells.)
    Do you typically purchase these products and/or
    services?

    (If yes) Would you be interested in an introduction,
    meeting, or discount coupon? [or offer whatever
    suits your business.]
    (If no) Thank you for your time.

At the end of the call (whether these B2B prospects answer yes or no), consider asking them to refer other businesses that use your types of products and services.

LOGO AND PRINTING TIPS

BONUS

A s I wrote this book, I realized that I couldn't exclude some basic information on... yes, logos, colors, and digital and print processes. I guarantee that gaining this knowledge and keeping it accessible will be very beneficial as you work on your company's marketing and branding strategies and tactics.

In the bonus material, I provide valuable terminology and processes for working with marketing and branding professionals and implementing your company's brand identity standards.

You can download this bonus material at: http://elainefogel.com/downloads/beyond-your-logo-bonus-material. Use this password: BYLBONUS.

If, for any reason, the landing page has moved, visit http://BeyondYourLogo.com for more information.

ACKNOWLEDGMENTS

M y sincerest gratitude goes to the Beta readers who volunteered to read the book draft and provide their feedback and recommendations. Thanks to Michelle Lydon, Mary Maxie, Mindy Sperber, Dale Walters, CPA, PFS, CFP®, and Harold Weiss.

A hearty thank you goes to my marketing pals and colleagues throughout North America — for their encouragement, support, feedback, and/or reviews: Iliana Arapis, Jay Baer, Jeanne Bliss, Toby Bloomberg, Carol Cone, Rachel Hutchisson, Shep Hyken, John Jantsch, Drew McLellan, Jeff Mendola, Omer Minkara, Dan Pink, Sybil Stershic, and Fran Tarkenton.

I also thank my friends in Canada and the US who graciously offered their feedback or assistance: Rachel Africa, Shahin Aghdasi, Bob Bercovici, Bina Feldman, Mike Flom, Michelle Lydon, Helen Meisel, Manfred Moennich, Barbara Ostroff, Hope Ozer, Ben Powers, Karen Ramsey, Ruth Slovitzer, Molly Spinak, Linda Walters, Sam Walters, and Zoë Maslow.

Lastly, I want to express my appreciation to my immediate family whose love, patience, and support have made me a better person.

THANK YOU!

ABOUT THE AUTHOR

E laine Fogel began her marketing career in her native Canada with agency freelance copywriting assignments for Procter & Gamble, Nestlé Carnation, and Kraft. Before relocating to the US, she held senior-level marketing positions at large organizations overseeing strategic brand building, integrated marketing communications, and customer service.

She is a professional speaker, marketing/branding thought leader, and president/CMO of Solutions Marketing & Consulting LLC in Scottsdale, Arizona. Elaine is a contributor to *SmallBizClub* (a joint project of Tarkenton Companies and Office Depot, Inc.) and her articles have appeared in many publications. People in 10 countries regularly read her blog, *Totally Uncorked on Marketing (elainefogel.net)*.

She has been a contributing writer for *The Business Journal* and *MarketingProfs*, and her content was included in three published books. Elaine's career has also included stints as a cookbook author, teacher, singer, and television show host.

In her "real life," she plays tennis, swims, follows a plant-based diet, and cuddles with her dogs, Mitzy and Snickers. She and her husband, Allen, became US citizens in 2014 and have two grown children.

Inquire about booking Elaine for an upcoming speaking or training engagement and sign up for her newsletter at elainefogel.com.

RESOURCES

All links were accessed in September 2015.

Aaker, David. *Aaker on Branding: 20 Principles That Drive Success*, New York: Morgan James Publishing, 2014

Accenture. *Accenture 2013 Global Consumer Pulse Survey: Global & U.S. Key Findings*, **https://www.accenture. com/t20150523T052453__w__/us-en/_acnmedia/ Accenture/Conversion-Assets/DotCom/Documents/ Global/PDF/Strategy_3/Accenture-Global-Consumer-Pulse-Research-Study-2013-Key-Findings. pdf;** "The $6 Trillion Opportunity: How Digital Can Improve Customer Experience to Drive Revenue Growth," Accenture Strategy, 2015, **http://www.accenture.com/us-en/ Pages/insight-digital-improve-customer-experience. aspx?c=strat_digicust_10000001&n=otc_0115**

Accenture/hybris. "Building The B2B OmniChannel Commerce Platform Of The Future, B2B Buyer Expectations Are Driving Sellers To Deliver Fully Functional Omni-Channel Experiences," November 2014, **https://www.accenture.com/il-en/ insight-building-b2b-omni-channel-commerce-platform-future.aspx**

Aflac. *2015 Aflac WorkForces Report*, Small company business trends, http://workforces.aflac.com/detailed-findings.php

American Express. *American Express® 2014 Global Customer Service Barometer, Findings in the United States*, **http:// about.americanexpress.com/news/docs/2014x/2014-Global-Customer-Service-Barometer-US.pdf**

Aon Hewitt. *2015 Trends in Global Employee Engagement*, **http://www.aon.com/human-capital-consulting/ thought-leadership/talent/2015-global-employee-engagement.jsp**

Baer, Jay. *Youtility*. New York: Penguin Group, 2013.

Baldoni, John. "Employee Engagement Does More than Boost Productivity," *Harvard Business Review*, July 4, 2013, **https://hbr.org/2013/07/employee-engagement-does-more/**

Boston College Carroll School of Management, Center for Corporate Citizenship. *State of Corporate Citizenship 2014*, **http://ccc.bc.edu/index.cfm?pageId=2928**

BusinessDictionary.com. "Market Reach," **http://www.businessdictionary.com/definition/market-reach.html**

Canadian Education and Research Institute for Counselling. *National Business Survey*, January 2014, **http://ceric.ca/career-development-in-the-canadian-workplace-national-business-survey/**

Cause Marketing Forum. "Background and Basics, Definition," **http://www.causemarketingforum.com/site/c.bkLUKcOTLkK4E/b.6443937/k.41E3/Background_and_Basics.htm**; "Statistics Every Cause Marketer Should Know," **http://www.causemarketingforum.com/site/c.bkLUKcOTLkK4E/b.6448131/k.262B/Statistics_Every_Cause_Marketer_Should_Know.htm**

Chaney, Paul. "My Small Business Social Media Training Manifesto," Chaney Marketing Group, June 18, 2012

CNN. "Turner, contractor to pay $2M in Boston bomb scare," February 5, 2007, **http://www.cnn.com/2007/US/02/05/boston.turner/index.html?eref=rss_us**

Cohn, Emily. "Stealing A Pen At Work Could Turn You On To Much Bigger Crimes," *The Huffington Post*, June 26, 2014, **http://www.huffingtonpost.com/2014/06/25/stealing-from-work-corporate-fraud_n_5530999.html**

Comcowich, William. "New Marketing Standard: Measure Online Ad Viewability, Not Impressions," *CyberAlert Blog*, May 13, 2014, **http://www.cyberalert.com/blog/index.php/new-marketing-standard-measure-online-ad-viewability-not-impressions/**

Cone Communications. *2015 Cone Communications/Ebiquity Global CSR Study*, http://www.conecomm.com/2015-cone-communications-ebiquity-global-csr-study

Connolly Properties. "How Does Your Workplace Environment Affect You?" *Healthy Beginnings Lifestyle Magazine*, http://hbmag.com/how-does-your-workplace-environment-affect-you

Content Marketing Institute. "What is Content Marketing?" http://contentmarketinginstitute.com/what-is-content-marketing/

Cornerstone OnDemand. "New Research Reveals Biggest Productivity Killers for America's Workforce," The State of Workplace Productivity Report, 2014, http://www.cornerstoneondemand.com/news/press-releases/new-research-reveals-biggest-productivity-killers-america%E2%80%99s-workforce

Culture Crossing Guide. http://guide.culturecrossing.net/

Customer Experience Matters. "Report: Employee Engagement Benchmark Study, 2015," *Temkin Employee Engagement Index*, February 17, 2015, https://experiencematters.wordpress.com/2015/02/17/report-employee-engagement-benchmark-study-2015/

Customer Service Psychology. "Customer Service Orientation," March 4, 2011, https://customerservicepsychology.wordpress.com/tag/customer-service-orientation-definition/

Daye, Derrick. "History of Branding," *Branding Strategy Insider*, August 14, 2006, http://www.brandingstrategyinsider.com/2006/08/history_of_bran.html#.UXB_ecJQh8E

Deloitte University Press. "Global Human Capital Trends 2014: Engaging the 21st-century workforce," http://dupress.com/wp-content/uploads/2014/04/GlobalHumanCapitalTrends_2014.pdf

DifferenceBetween.net. "Difference Between Offset and Digital Printing," **http://www.differencebetween.net/technology/difference-between-offset-and-digital-printing/**

Duffy, Jill. "Get Organized: How to Change Your Mobile Email Signature," *PCMag*, August 12, 2013, **http://www.pcmag.com/article2/0,2817,2422909,00.asp**

Edelman. *2014 Edelman Trust Barometer*, **http://www.edelman.com/insights/intellectual-property/2014-edelman-trust-barometer/about-trust/executive-summary/**

Edmunds, Adam. "Digging Deeper: How Emotions Drive Customer Choices," *E-Commerce Times*, November 22, 2008, **http://www.ecommercetimes.com/story/65251.html**

eMarketer. "How Will 2013's Digital Display Trends Converge in 2014?" February 18, 2014, **http://www.emarketer.com/Article/How-Will-2013rsquos-Digital-Display-Trends-Converge-2014/1010613**

Entrepreneur Media, Inc. "Return on Investment (ROI)," **http://www.entrepreneur.com/encyclopedia/return-on-investment-roi**; "Secondary Market Research," **http://www.entrepreneur.com/encyclopedia/secondary-market-research**; "Unique Selling Proposition (USP)," **http://www.entrepreneur.com/encyclopedia/unique-selling-proposition-usp**; "Your Brand's True Colors," **http://www.entrepreneur.com/article/175428**

Ethics Resource Center. "Ethical Leadership: Every Leader Sets a Tone," *National Business Ethics Survey*, 2014, **http://www.ethics.org/files/u5/ExecSummaryLeadership.pdf**

Gallup. "Americans Still More Confident in Small vs. Big Business," June, 2015, **http://www.gallup.com/poll/183989/americans-confident-small-big-business.aspx**

Gilroy, Kevin. "Agility At The Speed Of Small Business," *D!gitalist Magazine* by SAP, October 13, 2014, **http://www. digitalistmag.com/innovation/agility-at-speed-of-small-business-01573912**

Godin, Seth. "Define: Brand," *Seth's Blog*, December 13, 2009, **http://sethgodin.typepad.com/seths_blog/2009/12/ define-brand.html**

Goliger, Sarah. "The Essential Email Marketing Metrics You Should Be Tracking," *HubSpot Blog*, March 4, 2014, **http://blog.hubspot.com/marketing/metrics-email-marketers-should-be-tracking**

Goffgrafix.com. "Converting Pantone Colors to RGB." **http:// goffgrafix.com/pantone-rgb-100.php**

Grasshopper. "The Grasshopper Re-Brand: How We Did It and How It Went," **http://grasshopper.com/resources/ case-studies/grasshopper-rebranding/**

GreenBiz Group Inc. *State of Green Business 2014*, **https:// www.greenbiz.com/microsite/state-green-business/ state-green-business-report**

Greenpeace International. "The Trash Vortex," **http://www. greenpeace.org/international/en/campaigns/ oceans/pollution/trash-vortex/**

Greenstreet, Karyn. "What is a Mastermind Group? A Definition," The Success Alliance, **http://www.thesuccessalliance. com/what-is-a-mastermind-group.html**

Haberman, Michael. "Why Volunteering Is Good for your Business," *HuffPost Impact*, September 5, 2012, **http:// www.huffingtonpost.com/Michael-Haberman/ corporate-volunteering_b_1856314.html**

Harvard Kennedy School, Corporate Social Responsibility Initiative. **http://www.hks.harvard.edu/m-rcbg/CSRI/ init_main.html**

Hasselberger, Lynn. "22 Preposterous Facts about Plastic Pollution (And 10 Things We Can Do About It)," *EcoWatch*, April 7, 2014, **http://ecowatch.com/2014/04/07/22-facts-plastic-pollution-10-things-can-do-about-it/**

Hubspot. "The Art of Asking Survey Questions," **http://offers.hubspot.com/art-asking-survey-questions**

Hunt, Vivian, Layton, Dennis, Prince, Sara. "Diversity Matters," McKinsey & Company, November 2014, **http://www.mckinsey.com/insights/organization/why_diversity_matters**

Hussain, Anum. "CRM Expert Paul Greenberg Defines Customer Engagement," HubSpot Blogs, April 23, 2014, **http://blog.hubspot.com/sales/paul-greenberg-defines-customer-engagement**

Hutchisson, Rachel. "Creating an Employee Volunteer Program at Your Small Business," Blackbaud, Business Doing Good, 2014, **http://www.businessdoinggood.com/wp-content/uploads/03-14.CORP_.BizGood.CreatingVolunteerPlan.pdf**

Industry Canada. Small Business Branch, Key Small Business Statistics, August 2013, **https://www.ic.gc.ca/eic/site/061.nsf/vwapj/KSBS-PSRPE_August-Aout2013_eng.pdf/$FILE/KSBS-PSRPE_August-Aout2013_eng.pdf**

Internal Revenue Service (IRS). Publication 526, **http://www.irs.gov/publications/p526/ar02.html#en_US_2013_publink1000229649**

Investopedia. "Distribution Channel," **http://www.investopedia.com/terms/d/distribution-channel.asp**

Jackson, Jackie. "How to Determine Price in Each Marketing Structure in Terms of Maximizing Profit," *Houston Chronicle*, **http://smallbusiness.chron.com/determine-price-marketing-structure-terms-maximizing-profit-77971.html**

Jantsch, John. "The Definition of Branding," Duct Tape Marketing, November 7, 2007, **http://www.ducttapemarketing. com/blog/2007/11/07/the-definition-of-branding/**

Javascripter.net. "RGB-to-CMYK Color Conversion," **http:// www.javascripter.net/faq/rgb2cmyk.htm**; "RGB-to-Hex Conversion," **http://www.javascripter.net/faq/ rgbtohex.htm**

Jeffrey Gitomer's Sales Training Channel. "How Important Is Being Friendly" **http://youtu.be/LPzMEiw5XyM**

Josephson, Michael. "A Manager's Dilemma: Dealing with Misbehaving Top Performers," What Will Matter? Josephson Institute Center for Business Ethics, September 18, 2014, **http://whatwillmatter.com/2013/08/30/bonus-commentary-a-managers-dilemmadealing-with-mishaving-top-performers/**

Kentico. "Kentico Digital Experience Survey: Customer Trust in Content Marketing is High but Fragile," *Kentico Content Marketing Survey*, June 2, 2014, **http://www.kentico. com/Company/Press-Center/2014/Kentico-Digital-Experience-Survey-Customer-Trust-i**

Kingston University London. "Barclays-funded research finds a simple smile could be the key to business success," June 13, 2013, **http://www.kingston.ac.uk/news/article/1019/ 13-jun-2013-barclaysfunded-research-finds-a-simple simple-smile-could-be-the-key-to-business-success/**

Kline Weinreich, Nedra. *Hands-On Social Marketing: A Step-by-Step Guide to Designing Change for Good*, 2nd ed., Thousand Oaks, CA: Sage Publications, Inc., 2011.

Kotler, Philip, and Lee, Nancy. *Corporate Social Responsibility: Doing the Most Good for Your Company and Your Cause*, Hoboken, New Jersey: John Wiley & Sons, Inc., 2005.

Kourovskaia, Anastasia. "Increasing Brand Value: A Masterclass from the World's Strongest Brands," Millward Brown, 2013, http://www.millwardbrown.com/docs/default-source/insight-documents/articles-and-reports/Millward-Brown_Increasing-Brand-Value.pdf

Kreuser, Anne. "Boosting Employee Engagement Through Volunteerism," Edelman goodpurpose®, August 16, 2013, http://purpose.edelman.com/boosting-employee-engagement-through-volunteerism/

Kriss, Peter. "The Value of Customer Experience, Quantified," *Harvard Business Review*, August 1, 2014, https://hbr.org/2014/08/the-value-of-customer-experience-quantified

Leggett, Kate. "Navigate the Future of Customer Service in 2014," *Kate Leggett's Blog*, Forrester Research Inc., January 13, 2014, http://blogs.forrester.com/kate_leggett/14-01-13-forresters_top_trends_for_customer_service_in_2014

M2Talk.com. "Consumer Behaviors Towards Multi-Channel Customer Service," November 2014, http://www.slideshare.net/M2Talk/consumer-behaviors-towardsmultichannelcustomerservicegraphs

Making Measurement Make Sense (3MS), http://measurementnow.net/

Minkara, Omer. "Social Customer Care: Steps to Success in 2014," Aberdeen Group, August 2014, http://v1.aberdeen.com/launch/report/research_report/9571-RR-Social-CC-Strategy.asp

Monash University, Business and Economics. Marketing Dictionary, "Definition of customer loyalty," http://business.monash.edu/marketing/marketing-dictionary

National Business & Disability Council (NBDC). http://www.viscardicenter.org/services/nbdc/

Nazar, Jason. "16 Surprising Statistics About Small Businesses," *Forbes*, September 9, 2013, **http://www.forbes.com/ sites/jasonnazar/2013/09/09/16-surprising-statistics-about-small-businesses/**

Nelson, Audrey Ph.D. "Go Home and Put on Some Clothes: Has Casual Friday Gone Over the Top?" *He Speaks, She Speaks, Psychology Today*, March 8, 2010, **http:// www.psychologytoday.com/blog/he-speaks-she-speaks/201003/go-home-and-put-some-clothes-has-casual-friday-gone-over-the-top**

Newport, Frank. "Most U.S. Small-Business Owners Would Do It All Over Again," Gallup, *Wells Fargo/Gallup Small Business Index*, April 2014, **http://www.gallup.com/poll/169592/ small-business-owners-again.aspx**

Pantone Graphics. "Pantone Numbering Systems Explained," **http://www.pantone.com/pages/pantone/Pantone. aspx?pg=20051&ca=1**

Parature. *2014 State of Multichannel Customer Service Survey*, **http://ww2.parature.com/lp/report-2014-state-multichannel-cs-survey-comm.html**

Post, Tom. "The Surprising Secret Behind Small Business Success," *Forbes*, March 13, 2014, **http://www.forbes.com/sites/ tompost/2014/03/13/the-surprising-secret-behind-small-business-success/**

Preact CRM. "The 11 Step Plan for CRM Success," *CRM Software Blog*, July 14, 2014, **http://www.crmsoftwareblog. com/2014/07/the-11-step-plan-for-crm-success**

Reputation Institute. *2013 CSR RepTrak® 100 Study*, **http:// www.reputationinstitute.com/thought-leadership/ csr-reptrak-100**

Richardson, Adam "Understanding Customer Experience," Harvard Business Review, Oct. 28, 2010, **https://hbr. org/2010/10/understanding-customer-experie**

Rykrsmith, Eva. "Dress Code or Not, What You Wear Matters," *The Fast Track*, Intuit, May 23, 2012, **http://quickbase. intuit.com/blog/2012/05/23/dress-code-or-not-what-you-wear-matters/**

Schapiro Group, Inc., The. *The Real Value of Joining a Local Chamber of Commerce*, November 30, 2012; Battlecreek Area Chamber of Commerce. **http://www.battlecreek.org/downloads/ TheRealValueofJoiningaLocalChamber.pdf**

Schriever, Norm. "Plastic Water Bottles Causing Flood of Harm to Our Environment," *HuffPost Green*, September 28, 2013, **http://www.huffingtonpost.com/norm-schriever/ post_5218_b_3613577.html**

SearchQuotes.com. "Steve Brunkhorst Quotes & Sayings," **http:// www.searchquotes.com/quotes/author/Steve_ Brunkhorst/**; "Donald Porter Quotes," **http://www. searchquotes.com/quotes/author/Donald_Porter/**

Sharp, Isadore. *Four Seasons – The Story of a Business Philosophy*, Toronto: Penguin Books, 2009.

Sinberg, Laura. "What Not to Wear To Work," *Forbes*, July 22, 2009, **http://www.forbes.com/2009/07/22/office-fashion-sexy-forbes-woman-style-clothes.html**

Skrbina, Dena. "Blog Series Introduction: Consumers still prefer phone-based customer service, so don't let yours lag behind," *What's Next Blog*, Nuance, February 25, 2014, **http://whatsnext.nuance.com/consumers-prefer-conversational-phone-based-customer-service/**

Sluis, Sarah. "The 4 Pillars of Responsible Customer Engagement," *CRM Magazine*, April 2014, **http://www.destinationcrm. com/Articles/ReadArticle.aspx?ArticleID=95426**

Society for Human Resource Management. "2013 Employee Benefits: An Overview of Employee Benefits Offerings in the U.S.," *2013 SHRM Employee Benefits Survey*, June 2013, **http:// www.shrm.org/research/surveyfindings/articles/ documents/13-0245%202013_empbenefits_fnl.pdf**;

"Future Insights: The top trends for 2014 according to SHRM's HR subject matter expert panels," **https://www.shrm. org/Research/Documents/13-0724%202014%20 Panel%20Trends%20Report%20v3.pdf**

Society for Human Resource Management/Globoforce. "Employee Recognition Survey, Spring 2013 Report, Driving Stronger Performance Through Employee Recognition," **http:// go.globoforce.com/rs/globoforce/images/SHRM_ Spring2013_web.pdf**

Society for Imaging Sciences and Technology. "How a Printing Press Works," **http://www.imaging.org/ist/resources/ tutorials/printing_press.cfm**

Sorman, Audra. "The Best Way to Map the Customer Journey: Take a Walk in Their Shoes," *SurveyMonkey Blog*, March 21, 2014, **https://www.surveymonkey.com/blog/ en/blog/2014/03/21/map-customer-journey-keep-customers-happy/**

Sprynczynatyk, Rebecca and Parker, Andrea. "Customer surveys: How to Raise Your Sales & Marketing IQ in 6 Easy Steps," Infusionsoft, **http://www.infusionsoft.com/resources/ ebook/how-raise-your-sales-marketing-iq-6-easy-steps**

Srivastava, Rajendra and Metz Thomas, Greg. "The Executive's Guide to Branding – Corporate Performance and Brands: The Risk and Return Effects of Branding," *Zyman Institute of Brand Science – Perspectives*, Zyman Institute of Brand Science, Goizueta Business School at Emory University, 2005, **http://www.zibs.com/GuidetoBranding.pdf**

Statistics Canada. *Canadian Survey on Disability, 2012,* **http:// www.statcan.gc.ca/pub/89-654-x/89-654-x2013001-eng.htm**

Stelzner, Michael A. "2015 Social Media Marketing Industry Report: How Marketers Are Using Social Media To Grow Their Businesses," *Social Media Examiner*, http://www.socialmediaexaminer.com/SocialMediaMarketingIndustryReport2015.pdf

Stengel, Jim. *Grow: How Ideals Power Growth and Profit at the World's Greatest Companies*, New York: Crown Business, 2011.

Sternberg, Robert. "Ethical Drift," Liberal Education, Association of American Colleges & Universities, http://www.aacu.org/liberaleducation/le-su12/sternberg.cfm

Sun, Wenbin PhD. "Does Corporate Social Responsibility Save Firms? An Exploration of Corporate Social Responsibility, Firm Capability, Environmental Influences, and Firm Default Risk," AMA Summer Educators' Conference Proceedings; 2012, Vol. 23, p247, January 2012.

Think Beyond the Label, "Tools for Success: The Business Case," http://www.thinkbeyondthelabel.com/Learning-Tools/BusinessCase.aspx

TinyHR. 2014 *TINYpulse Employee Engagement and Organizational Culture Report*, http://www.tinyhr.com/2014-employee-engagement-organizational-culture-report

Towers Watson. *2014 Global Workforce Study at a Glance*, August 2014, http://www.towerswatson.com/en-US/Insights/IC-Types/Survey-Research-Results/2014/08/the-2014-global-workforce-study

Tran, Charles. "Survey: Customer Service Statistics," CreditDonkey, July 3, 2013, http://www.creditdonkey.com/customer-service-2013.html

Transportation Research Board, Commercial Truck and Bus Safety Synthesis Program. "Impact of Behavior-Based Safety Techniques on Commercial Motor Vehicle Drivers," 2007, http://onlinepubs.trb.org/onlinepubs/ctbssp/ctbssp_syn_11.pdf

UnitedHealth Group. *Doing Good is Good for You 2013 Health and Volunteering Study*, **http://www.unitedhealthgroup. com/~/media/UHG/PDF/2013/UNH-Health-Volunteering-Study.ashx**

United States Bureau of Labor Statistics, Division of Labor Force Statistics. "Employment status of the civilian noninstitutional population by disability status and selected characteristics, 2013 annual averages," **http://www.bls.gov/news. release/disabl.to1.htm**; Occupational Safety & Health Administration, "Safety and Health Add Value," https://**www. osha.gov/Publications/safety-health-addvalue.html**

United States Small Business Administration, Office of Advocacy. "Frequently Asked Questions about Small Businesses," March 2014, **http://www.sba.gov/sites/default/files/FAQ_ March_2014_0.pdf**

Vitez, Osmond, "Meaning of Professionalism and Work Ethic," *Houston Chronicle*, **http://smallbusiness.chron.com/ meaning-professionalism-work-ethic-746.html**

Wells Fargo Works for Small Business. "Small business optimism is at a six year high," 2014, **https://wellsfargoworks.com/ q4-2014-small-business-index-infographic**

WhatIs.com. "Definition brand," June 2010, **http://whatis. techtarget.com/definition/brand**

Wikipedia. "Belief System," **http://en.wikipedia.org/wiki/ Belief_system**; "Digital Printing," **http://en.wikipedia. org/wiki/Digital_printing**; "HSL and HSV," **http:// en.wikipedia.org/wiki/HSL_and_HSV**; "Offset Printing," **http://en.wikipedia.org/wiki/Offset_printing**; "Print on Demand," **http://en.wikipedia.org/wiki/Print_on_ demand**; "RGB Color Model," **http://en.wikipedia.org/ wiki/RGB**; "SMART criteria," **http://en.wikipedia.org/ wiki/SMART_criteria**; "Variable Data Printing,"

http://en.wikipedia.org/wiki/Variable_data_
printing; "Vector Graphics," http://en.wikipedia.org/wiki/
Vector_graphics; "Web Colors," http://en.wikipedia.
org/wiki/Web_colors; "Appreciative Inquiry," http://
en.wikipedia.org/wiki/Appreciative_inquiry

Williams, Jed and Campbell, Kristy. "Achieving Big Customer
Loyalty in a Small Business World," *Manta & BIA/
Kelsey Customer Loyalty Surveys*, January 2014, http://
wordpress-src.s3.amazonaws.com/wp-content/
uploads/BiaMantaKelsey-SBloyalty.pdf

Workforce Mood Tracker. "Spring 2014 Report, Adapting to
the Realities of Our Changing Workforce," Globoforce,
http://go.globoforce.com/rs/globoforce/images/
Spring2014MoodTrackerGloboforce.pdf

Zendesk/Dimensional Research. "Customer Service and
Business Results," April 2013, https://d16cvnquvjw7pr.
cloudfront.net/resources/whitepapers/Zendesk_
WP_Customer_Service_and_Business_Results.pdf

Zywien, Josh. "Redefining Customer Engagement: Ogilvy
Marketing Executive Rohit Bhargava on Why Modern
Marketing Tactics Mostly Come Up Short," OpenView Sales
Lab, July 24, 2012, http://labs.openviewpartners.com/
redefining-customer-engagement-qa-with-rohit-
bhargava/

INDEX